REGENERATIVE
PURPOSE

The Dynamic Nature
of the Way We Choose Work

WENDY MAY

Note from the author

The digital e-book and audiobook files are provided without copy restriction, in trust. Each electronic download is intended for one household.

You can share freely with the humans that you share intimate space with. Please do not send or share the digital files of *Regenerative Purpose* outside of the circle of immediate family and/or housemates. (If the boundaries of this circle are unclear, imagine the people you would choose to be in a quarantine bubble with.)

Files that take only 15 seconds to download are borne from more than 15 months of emotional and intellectual devotion. If the receivers who benefit from this work contribute a few dollars each to this creation, that collective energy nourishes me and allows me to continue my purpose work.

Please share, with integrity

Recommend *Regenerative Purpose* by directing friends and other connections to my website to obtain their copy. Thank you for your support!

— Wendy May
heywendymay.com

Table of Contents

Foreword

There is an apocalyptic undertone to Wendy May's vital contribution to the body of work on the matter of purpose. We live at a critical juncture in human history, and it is more important than ever that we decide how to exercise our humanity and choose how to walk in this world.

There are plenty of books on purpose, some worth reading, many proffering a shopworn sequence of platitudes that you've heard before, in the manner of stylized memes on one's Facebook feed. One might pause before writing a book on a subject which the author suggests from the outset is ubiquitous. *Regenerative Purpose* delivers an important new voice to the conversation, and a compelling new prescription.

I had the privilege of witnessing the early gestation of Wendy's fresh approach to the topic at a writer's retreat that I hosted. I closed the event with some words on the notion of purpose and visioning. Wendy asked to add commentary, and after receiving my consent, proceeded to do a second close with a fierce delivery of her own thoughts on the subject.

We both have ties to the San Francisco Bay Area and now live on Koh Phangan, having left behind careers in corporate America in favor of the bohemian, nature-rich, creative environment of island living. Once she began writing her book, I saw Wendy at cafes around the island from time to time, deeply absorbed, as she worked away at her first draft.

When she engaged me to review those early chapters, I was astounded at the clarity and vitality of her work. I was familiar with her Kaistara project ("embodied purpose coaching and retreats for humans on their soul purpose path," quite a promise), so I knew of her years formulating, testing, and practicing her perspectives. But this book, which you hold in your hands, forcefully crystallizes those ideas, achieving the difficult alchemy of delivering a big think with grace, warmth, and accessible language.

On virtually every page, I found myself pausing for one of three reasons:

1. I recognized the idea, but I had never seen it expressed in such a practical and actionable manner.
2. I recognized the idea, but I was seeing for the first time how it related to certain struggles or passages in my life.
3. I read something entirely new, which helped me make fresh sense of my life and work.

You have a treat in store. A great read, a steady stream of new thinking on a subject critical to making wise and principled choices, and a contemporary, and thus immediately relevant bit of inspiration.

I too lived what Wendy calls the "fake plant life," and I loved it, raised a family with it, am grateful for all of it. And then, I too examined it more closely and came to ask myself some tough questions. I wish I had had this book 25 years ago, but I didn't have the privilege.

You do, dear reader, and I wish you great joy and moments of awe and wonder as you suck the marrow out of every page.

Brian Gruber

CHAPTER 1

Starting on the Purpose Path

There is now a single issue before us: survival. Not merely physical survival, but survival in a world of fulfilment, survival in a living world, where the violets bloom in the springtime, where the stars shine down in all their mystery, survival in a world of meaning.
— **Thomas Berry**

W e are preoccupied with purpose these days. Organizations struggle to articulate their purpose to an increasingly purpose-seeking workforce. We speculate about the rise of the purpose economy. We network with like-minded social entrepreneurs at purpose summits. We take online quizzes to help us diagnose our purpose. In other words, purpose is the new black.

The idea that humans are naturally pulled towards purpose or meaning is not exactly breaking news. Thinkers have been examining this question for eons. As a species, we are fascinated with the exploration of why we exist. We are curious about what moves us to do what we do. We want to understand the mysterious impulse that motivates us to look beyond personal success or personal survival. This inquiry is really nothing new.

So why I am writing this book, and why now?

We are alive at a critical point in the story of humanity. It is a time of intensity, uncertainty, and mind-bending paradox.

Some are enjoying an unprecedented level of prosperity, health, and convenience in modern life, while others face persistent hardship and injustice.

We have access to technology that can automatically pilot cars, genetically clone sheep, and reliably predict our buying behavior. At the same time, families and communities are more and more fragmented; anxiety and depression are on the rise; and mass violence has become a frighteningly common way to vent frustration with society's ills. We are obsessed with consuming, and yet we never feel full. We are masterful with technology, and yet we suffer so much disease.

Many of our long-held institutions are being confronted and challenged. Our social and economic structures stand ripe for revolution. Every aspect of life as we know it is being called into question. We are in the midst of a massive transformation that touches every dimension of human existence — including financial markets, political systems, media channels, education models, food sources, relationship structures, and more. The old paradigm is collapsing and what's coming next is not completely clear. The new paradigm is not yet here. We feel a sense of disidentification and dislocation as we hover in the in-between. It's uncomfortable.

It's no wonder that our desire for purpose has intensified with all this uncertainty and turmoil. And yet, a word of caution. Purpose is a possible way out of this mess, but it can also become part of the problem.

I met my friend Kim for lunch one day while I was brainstorming ideas for a book title. Kim is a lifelong student of linguistics. As we chatted, she reminded me that words do not have absolute meaning, only the meanings we assign them.

Words are merely the modern-day evolution of hand gestures and hieroglyphics. They are the millionth iteration of crude stick figures scratched on cave walls by early humans. "Hey I saw this thing. Did you also see it?" "Yes, we both saw the same thing." "I just ate this thing." "Oh, can we eat this thing?"

I thought about the word "purpose" as I reflected on this. And I considered some other words that are now trending — patriarchal, feminine, sovereign, intersectional, and conscious, for example. It seems that when a word gains popularity, the meanings that it can carry will multiply. Along with the increase in the number of interpretations, there comes an expansion in possible misuses and potential miscommunication.

We need to be careful about the distortion of purpose as it becomes common in mainstream consciousness. Purpose is at risk of becoming another coveted possession that is used to trigger our seeking and buying behavior. We are offered courses that objectify purpose as an outcome. We see advertisements that use purpose-lack and purpose-shame to motivate action.

We are called upon to not fall into seeking purpose the same way we have pursued material wealth, social status, or power over others. To create a whole new paradigm of purpose, we must shift *how* we do things, not just *what* we do. If we fail at making that shift, then purpose loses its potency; it will just end up being the same old salad, with new-age dressing.

Living the fake plant life

This book is more personal missive than it is personal memoir. Yet before we dive into the details of regenerative purpose, I want to set the context for our exploration by giving you a brief glimpse into my own purpose journey.

By the time I reached my mid-30s, I was winning at life according to most traditional measures of success. I had degrees from top-ranked universities. I had a resume full of impressive job titles at highly-respected companies. I was a director at a prestigious global consulting firm. I owned a beautiful one-bedroom condo in a nice neighborhood in San Francisco.

It was a fake plant kind of life. It was bright, shiny, and smooth; it looked perfect when gazing from afar. Looking up close though, there was a sense of aliveness that was missing. What was missing from my life was the radiance of realness.

I remember the day when a senior partner at my consulting firm kept me on the phone after a conference call. (This is basically the grown-up equivalent of being held by the teacher after school.) He asked, "What's going on with you, Wendy? I am not feeling the warm fuzzies from you." A wide array of thoughts and emotions whirled through me in that moment: indignation, anger, defensiveness, and eventually, recognition and acceptance. He was right. I was not feeling it — whatever "it" is that I wanted to be feeling.

Taking a hard look, I could see how my high-maintenance lifestyle was making me feel exhausted and frustrated. I was hustling to feed this Frankenstein's monster — this competitive, consumption-driven existence — and it was not nourishing me in return. I was longing for deeper meaning, but I had no idea how I could access it. My life up to that point had been focused on achieving financial security. I had no idea how to do anything else. I had no idea how to change. The only thing that I knew for sure was that this was no longer what I wanted to be doing with my "one wild and precious life."

Since then, I have been on a roller-coaster ride of rediscovering and reimagining what my life is for. I have served in temporary contractor roles, taken on independent consulting gigs, and worked with many executive coaching clients. I have held intimate retreats for women in career transition. I have invested thousands of dollars in training and personal development experiences for myself. I have started an online business selling biodegradable glitter. By the time you read this, I will have published a book.

I have done many things, but I am not done. I definitely do not have everything all figured out. My life is not pure adventure, beauty, and bliss. On many days, it feels like hard work. The difference is that nowadays I wake up feeling aligned, alive, and engaged with life — even when things are challenging. The way I see it, purpose is not about uncovering a hidden assignment that you have to complete; it is about becoming more available to serve in each waking moment.

I didn't know that I was on a purpose journey when I started out. It was only later that I came to know the impulse that was moving me by the name of purpose. What I learned along the way is that purpose is an expression of human nature. Yet purpose is not passive. Purpose doesn't just happen when we are sleepwalking. It doesn't fall out of the sky into our lap when we are wishing on a star. Purpose *wants* to happen *through* us, but we also have to choose it. We consciously give consent to allow our life to be used as a vehicle for something bigger than us. When we choose to walk the purpose path, it requires our active awareness, commitment, and engagement.

That is what this book is about. It is about how you can intentionally step into the embodied experience of purpose and establish this as your new normal.

How to use this book

As Bruce Lee advised, "Use no way as way. When there is a 'Way' therein lies the limitation. When there is a circumference, it traps. And if it traps, it rots. And if it rots, it is lifeless." So, in other words, I am not here to show you the way. What I hope to do is introduce several possible ways for you to explore.

Some of my ideas may bring clarity; others may beget confusion. In this book, I take on certain positions to challenge the current paradigm. Once published, these words are static, but the nature of life is dynamic. Even in the time that it takes for me to write this book, our cultural center of gravity around purpose is shifting. One day, some of the stances that I take in this book might seem unnecessarily extreme. For now, I believe they are illustrative and intentionally provocative; they are designed to challenge conventional wisdom. You may disagree with me or feel uncomfortable with some of what I am sharing and you are invited to pay attention to all of that. There is important information for you enclosed in those reactions.

I don't have a five-step formula for fulfillment to sell you. This is not an instruction manual to teach you how to replicate my life's path. Even if you were excellent at following directions, once you managed to get the whole thing assembled you would likely discover that what you had built doesn't fit you. Purpose is far too fickle to have a formula.

My opinions are colored by my personal circumstances. The perspectives I share are sourced from my personal experiences. I am human and imperfect and growing, just like you. And my insights are biased from my viewpoint of relative privilege.

Please don't do as I say. In fact, don't even do as I do. What has worked for me may not work for you. Equally, please resist the temptation to discard what I am offering here because you see all the ways that I am different from you.

As the reader, you need to be engaged in filtering and translating the ideas in this book into what is personally meaningful and relevant for you. You are invited to look at what is here and extract what is useful for you.

I encourage you to be your own guru and access your own inner teacher. Take away what you find helpful here and leave the rest behind. Use these words to spark your own investigation. These concepts that I present here are not meant to be swallowed whole as the light of absolute truth.

Ultimately, this book is a form that I have created to express purpose in a particular moment of my life. I am grateful that you have decided to join me for this part of the adventure.

CHAPTER 2

Introducing a New Paradigm of Purpose

We are already what we seek, and what we are looking for on the Path with such an intensity of striving and passion and discipline is already within and around us at all moments.

— Andrew Harvey

When we make contact with another human for the first time, our "sorting hat" is on. On a subconscious level, we silently assign categories to the people we meet. We make quick judgements and sort and label them so we can get on with the business of relating with them based on past experience with similarly-sorted humans. On a basic level, we want to know: Friend or foe? Trustworthy or not trustworthy? Capable or not capable?

We can sort people according to the neighborhood they live in, the car they drive, or the clothes they wear. When we meet someone new and they ask us, "What do you do?", they are sorting. With this question, they might be curious to learn our rank, title, or salary; they might be looking for a clue about our education, interests, or values. We can also sort people according to purpose. We ask: "What do you care most about?" or "What is your deepest passion?" or "What is your life mission?"

Many of my coaching clients confess to being triggered by such questions. They report feeling an uneasiness that *I don't know what my purpose is but I feel like I should.* When we are faced with the innocent open-ended question: "What is your purpose?" there is often another underground assessment that is taking place: "Do you even have a purpose? Why don't you know what it is?" Feelings of confusion and shame can arise as we wrestle with the purpose dilemma. The discomfort this brings makes it tempting to look outside for answers.

Purpose for sale

When we sort based on purpose, we separate people into categories of "purpose haves" and "purpose have-nots." In doing this, we treat purpose as an object of seeking. It is something that you have or do not have — and if you do not have it, you are somehow lacking it and wanting it. When we see purpose as an objective, we adopt a linear, strategic, and goal-oriented approach to reaching it. We play the game of life with purpose as an achievement to unlock. Where money, status, and power may have once been the desired ends to our efforts, now it has become more fashionable to pursue purpose as the ultimate prize instead.

We talk about *finding* or *figuring out* our life purpose. We talk about following the breadcrumb trail of our passions to reach it as if purpose is hidden somewhere "out there" in the wilderness. We talk about uncovering or revealing our purpose, as though purpose can be found "in there" somewhere, buried beneath a secret trap door in our psyche. The language of heroic quest supports the belief that purpose requires a search. We see it as something to seek and find, something to know and name.

We treat purpose as our prey to hunt and capture; our treasure to discover and recover; or our trophy to drag back to our cave and mount on the wall.

This objectification of purpose is cause for caution. Whenever there is a desired object that we believe we have or do not have, a lineup of people will be waiting to sell us the thing that we feel we are missing. We are bombarded with ads for secret guides to fulfillment or simple blueprints for a meaningful life. Purpose has become a new age award of significance; it is yet another marker of "having your shit together."

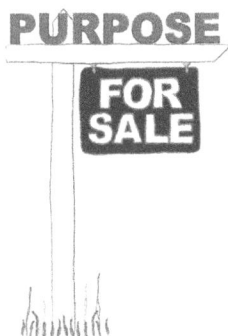

When we sort people into groups of "purpose haves" and "purpose have-nots," we introduce a power dynamic. We buy into the myth that some have the keys to the kingdom and others do not. If you want access, you can buy a membership pass. These offers lure us with the promise of simplicity and certainty. So-called experts use scarcity and disempowerment to sell us an "easy-button" for our heart's desires. These classic marketing tactics are as old as dirt — the only difference now is that the object for sale is purpose.

Purpose, reimagined

We need to make space for a more fluid, more dynamic, more creative, more receptive, and more regenerative approach to purpose. The new way is one that respects purpose as a force of nature. It is about enlivening ourselves as an expression of nature and aligning with the rhythms and cycles of that nature.

To support our shift into the new paradigm of purpose work, I am proposing five key reframes of commonly held notions around purpose:

1. Purpose is not an objective; it is a practice
2. Purpose is not singular; it is multifaceted
3. Purpose is not definitive; it is dynamic
4. Purpose is not personal; it is relational
5. Purpose is not a form; it is an experience

1. Purpose is not an objective; it is a practice

What if there is no pot of gold at the end of the rainbow? Western, goal-directed, linear logic treats purpose as an endpoint. In this outdated paradigm, once we discover what our purpose is, it becomes the object of a strategic plan to achieve it. There is this idea that once we finally accomplish this goal, then everything will be hunky-dory. We will be able to relax once we get there, because then *we have arrived*.

In the new paradigm, purpose is not the promised land to reach so we can retire. There is no resting place called purpose. It is an ever-evolving, always unfolding, lifelong adventure. Purpose is not the final destination. In fact, purpose serves us best when we use it as a compass for re-orientation.

Purpose is not a single-serving, life-defining choice. It acts more like guardrails for the ongoing series of decisions, one after the next, which gradually define the course of our lives. This way purpose becomes a practice. We need to practice purpose daily, weekly, monthly — the same way we practice yoga asanas, mindfulness meditation, or acts of kindness. When we stop pursuing a single life purpose and start living on purpose, our worldview changes. We move away from purpose as an objective and start to embrace purpose as a practice.

PURPOSE ~~IS AN OBJECTIVE~~ IS practice

2. Purpose is not singular; it is multifaceted

When we talk about purpose, we usually focus on the purpose of the work we do. That focus is often further limited to the work we do to earn our living. Yes, we complete tasks and perform jobs to secure our livelihood but that is only one dimension of our life. Purpose covers a much broader territory than that. We can also be purposeful in how we show affection to our partner, give advice to our children, organize community outings, make watercolor paintings, smile at the supermarket cashier, or pick up trash on the beach. All of this in a day's work.

Imagine how our existence touches a multitude of other individuals, groups, and systems during the span of our lifetimes. Our purpose is a direct reflection of our inner work as much as it is a result determined by our outer work. In this way, purpose work is an expression of love that touches everyone and everything that we touch in the course of our lives. It is not restricted to the domain of our work-life.

PURPOSE
~~IS SINGULAR~~
IS MULTIFACETED

3. Purpose is not definitive; it is dynamic

Another misconception around purpose is perpetuated by what I refer to as "encoded mission rhetoric". Motivational speakers often say things like, "You were born for a reason," or "You are here for a purpose." These inspiring catchphrases are misleading because they suggest that we carry some invisible mission that is written into our DNA. The strange thing is, when this secret life assignment was supposedly handed out at birth, it was also hidden from our view. The idea is that we must try to uncover this mysterious, predetermined purpose of ours before we die.

And if we cannot manage to decode our hidden destiny, we may be doomed to waste our lives.

Purpose is real, but it is not solid. Trying to capture it feels like chasing a rainbow. As soon as you approach the place where you think it ends, it moves; it changes; it shape-shifts. We exist within a fast spinning global vortex of ideas, resources, cultures, communities, economies, ecosystems, and technologies. We live in an instantaneous feedback loop with these forces. And in the same moment that they are shaping our thoughts, feelings, and actions, these external influences are themselves evolving. Even if we managed to pin down our purpose, it would fly away again as soon as we turned around.

PURPOSE
IS ~~definitive~~
IS Dynamic
—

4. Purpose is not personal; it is relational

Purpose becomes easily entangled with our sense of identity. If we find a way to name it, we might be tempted to wear it as a badge or make it into a brand. We often adopt a purpose label for ourselves in our pursuit of significance. We mistake purpose for something personal, something that is *ours* to own and hold. We try to define it and describe it. We want to claim it.

New paradigm purpose, however, emerges from the relational field between the individual and the collective. This purpose exists only in the space of conversation between you and the rest of the world. If you are not open and engaged with your reality — if you are only talking to and about yourself — then you are missing the point of purpose.

From your personal perspective, purpose work makes you feel expressed, engaged, rewarded, and fulfilled. From a broader perspective, purpose work is where you are best used as an instrument to serve the greater good. True purpose has both these faces. It reveals itself in the interplay of the individual and the collective. Ultimately, your purpose doesn't belong to you. In a sense, it is not really "yours." It cannot exist in isolation — it only comes to life when there is an ongoing conversation between you and the world.

PURPOSE
~~is personal~~
is relational

5. Purpose is not a form; it is an experience

What does someone who is "on purpose" look like? Is it someone who is healthy and vibrant? Someone with a sleek website highlighting an inspiring mission statement? Someone who lives in a minimalist tiny home? Someone with a massive, ardent social media following? Someone who is "crushing it" financially? Someone who works remotely while drinking fresh coconuts on the beach? Someone who leaves a bevy of enlightened beings in their wake?

Maybe purpose doesn't look like anything at all. The subjective experience of purpose is independent of form; it is not tied to any structure in physical reality — not a business, not a brand, not a barn house. Purpose is an inside job; the only person who can truly tell you if you are on purpose is *you*. No one else really knows. The impressions registered by others from outside are unreliable at best, and misleading at worst.

Purpose has nothing to do with having a corporate job or being an entrepreneur; nothing to do with living in a big city or living in a remote mountain cabin. There are plenty of public figures who look quite successful on social media, but are still strangers to the experience of purpose. Don't be fooled by the form — our internal states of disconnection and dis-ease are rarely featured on the public stage. It is possible to be lit up with the ecstatic experience of purpose flow without moving an inch on the outside. You only need to be willing to move mountains on the inside.

The essence of purpose is timeless and formless. Like all things that manifest in the material world, the shapes that purpose takes on are only temporary. We need to approach the various purpose forms that we create from an orientation of stewardship, rather than ownership. Sometimes purpose may take a form that lasts a short time; other times it may create something that endures or even outlives us. On the other hand, purpose can also be fulfilled in a formless fleeting encounter, like the one my friend Katie Mae had on a train ride:

I was on a train somewhere in the heart of Texas, on my way to Arizona. After sleeping through the night, the clickety-clack of the train that had lulled me to sleep was interrupted by the voice of the man in the seat behind me.

"You're so stupid," he said. "You can't do anything right. I don't know how you're going to raise this baby when you're so stupid that you can't even take care of basic shit."

I stood up from my seat and looked behind me to see an angry man talking on his phone. I gave him a look of shocked disgust before sitting back down. He fell silent for a while.

I had no idea who he was talking to, but I knew that no one deserved to be spoken to that way. I tried to distract myself by reading a book but I couldn't shake it.

It started up again, quieter this time. "I can't believe you fucked this up too. You're so stupid. This baby is fucked."

My skin crawled. I packed up my things as the torrent of abuse continued, shot him another look of disdain, and changed train cars. My body was shaking and my cheeks were flushed. I didn't know what to do. I wanted to say something to him. It felt both right and terrifying. He was obviously a very angry person. Did I really want to subject myself to that? Maybe it was best to just mind my own business.

A few hours passed, and I couldn't stop thinking about

what I'd heard, and wondering who the woman was on the other end. I felt like I needed to say something, but I was also nervous.

I decided to leave it up to fate. A couple of hours had passed since I'd changed trains. Maybe he'd gotten off. If he was still on the train, I would take it as a sign to say something. If not, I could let it go knowing there was nothing I could do.

So, I went back to the other train car and there he was. There was an empty seat next to him. I asked him if I could sit down, and he agreed. I smiled and introduced myself. I told him I couldn't help but overhear his conversation that morning, and asked who he'd been talking to. He was talking to a woman who was pregnant with his child. She was going to have his baby soon, and he was traveling outside the Midwest for the first time in his life to be there for the birth. She was supposed to pick him up at the station but couldn't for some reason, and that's why he was so upset with her. I listened to him. I could see that he was afraid.

After he finished speaking, I looked him in the eye and said, "What I overheard was abuse. No one deserves to be spoken to that way. I understand you're nervous about arriving in a new city, but that doesn't give you the right to speak like that. Whatever a mother experiences, the baby also experiences, so all that abuse is damaging your child, too. Do you care about this baby?"

He assured me he did. I believed him. I steered the conversation toward ways to communicate frustration without becoming abusive. I explained that being unable to borrow a vehicle did not make the woman "stupid" and that it was not her responsibility to alleviate his fear. I reassured him that he would be fine when he arrived in Dallas. Before I left, we shared a long hug. When I said goodbye, we were both relaxed and smiling.

I doubt that that moment was a complete turnaround in his life, but I felt better after saying something, and I think it had some influence on him. I hope his baby's life is a little better because of it.

When Katie Mae shared this story with me, it struck me as a great example of how our purpose can be called into creation in a moment in time and concluded in the same moment, without ever taking a form that can be named and labeled. Purpose happens when a need that we are uniquely equipped to serve presents itself to us, and we are present enough to respond.

PURPOSE ~~IS FORM~~ IS Experience

If purpose can be formed and formless, then the task at hand is both strikingly simple and challenging. Instead of setting our sights on finding *a* purpose, we must engage in living *on* purpose. Regenerative purpose asks us to show up for life in a different way: true, present, loving, attentive, responsive, and available to serve. Purpose work is never complete. We never graduate from the school of purpose. It is something we choose to engage in over and over again, as long as we live. The art of living in alignment with purpose becomes our life's work.

How to recognize purpose

If purpose is not an object, not singular, not fixed, not personal, and not a form, then what is it? No short definition suffices. I can only share a number of views, which — when combined — point us toward a sense of what being *on purpose* feels like. From my own experience and interviews with others, four themes emerged around how we experience purpose alignment.

1. I feel good about being myself
2. I feel good about helping others
3. I experience ease in taking action
4. I experience magic and feel supported

I feel good about being myself

I feel good about helping others

I experience ease in taking action

I experience "magic" and feel supported

I feel good about being myself

Nearly every person that I interviewed for this book mentioned that purpose work is pleasurable. Part of the experience of being *on purpose* is that it feels liberating or uplifting on a personal level. Some describe purpose work bringing forth a sense of freedom to reveal their true selves. Some say purpose gives rise to a positive emotion akin to satisfaction or happiness. Others suggest purpose often comes with a frequency of ease or sweetness. In these ways, we see how purpose alignment naturally evokes enjoyment in self-expression.

Work feels more purposeful to me when I enjoy doing it. It's not that purpose is necessarily synonymous with satisfaction or happiness, but doing my purpose is something that makes me happy.
— **Michael Duff, information security executive**

I know when I am on purpose when I am in my full expression. I know that I am in it when I can show my true self. I experience a lot of energy in my system and I feel good about everything that is going on.
— **Ann Liu, painter**

There's a level of sincerity and honesty that is needed in living your purpose. It's important to stay true to your guiding principles. Being authentic and open with people about what we're trying to do is critical.
— **Nehal Vadhan, psychologist**

I feel good about helping others

Another theme that arose in my interviews was the idea of healing or helping others. Some referred to the satisfaction they derive from using their own life lessons to provide guidance for others. Other people spoke about feeling a strong motivation to be in service or answering a calling to have a greater impact. In other words, when we are aligned with purpose work, we often recognize the broader benefit of our efforts and remember that we are contributing to something beyond ourselves.

I want to help other people, especially women, to embrace and enjoy sex. I have always loved sex.
Yet there was wounding from the unconscious use of my sexuality. It was part of my own evolution to move past purely physical sex, to sex as spiritual union. And now what I can do to contribute to the world is help other people make the same transition.
— Martha Lee, clinical sexologist

One aspect of purpose is the impact it has on the people around me. I feel a sense of purpose when my work is impactful. I want to know that it changes the world or has a positive effect on people in some way.
— Michael Duff

Purpose is something that gets you out of bed in the morning — especially for me, because I'm a night owl. I'm not a scientist by nature, so sometimes I struggle at work. But my work gives me purpose because I can see that it has a global impact.
— Matteo Ottaviani, climate research scientist

I experience ease in taking action

Those familiar with the feeling of being *on purpose* frequently mention experiencing flow states. They report having episodes of hyperfocus where time seems to disappear and personal energy seems to expand. There is a quality of ease associated with participating in purpose-aligned action. In this flow state, the act of creation unfolds naturally and effortlessly, rather than through striving to be productive. Progress is apparent without the need for any pushing.

> *I know when I am aligned with my purpose because things just start to flow. I don't have to make a huge effort. I don't have to push to make things happen.*
> — **Amanda Johnson, author mentor**

> *You know how when we are in flow states, we lose the concept of time? Purpose is like that for me. When I am in my purpose world, I lose track of how many hours it has been. I can keep going and going and going.*
> — **Ann Liu**

> *When I feel inspired about doing something, it's probably part of my purpose. When I am feeling aligned and uplifted, and in the flow, I know I am on purpose.*
> — **Nick Williams, inspired leadership guide**

I experience "magic" and feel supported

The fourth and final theme that came from my interviews is the awareness of an ever-present fabric of support. In the state of being *on purpose*, there is a shared experience of being held, being guided, being connected, and being supported by everything around us. We sense an invisible web that is always holding us up and holding us together. Many relayed that this support often feels magical or mysterious because it arrives on its own accord, unplanned and unbidden by the receiver.

Lately, I am starting to experience purpose more and more as a sense of faith. I feel like I have these universal arms that are wrapped around me, holding me. There's a magical quality to feeling on purpose. The way things are occurring, somehow, I find myself in exactly the right place at exactly the right time, without any explanation.
— **Brandon Peele, purpose guide**

The first time I experienced a sense of purpose, I was doing a biofeedback study on pilots' stress responses in emergency situations. I incorporated a meditation technique, which helped the pilots get a better handle on their fight or flight mechanism. A lot of synchronicities started happening then. I was receiving opportunities and invitations to events. I had a strong feeling that this was something I was here to do.
— **Daan Gorter, social entrepreneurship mastermind creator**

Everything has started to move effortlessly now, without me grasping or trying to make things happen. Clients are finding me. Work is getting done on time. I am receiving credible feedback and praise. It is magical.
— **Amanda Johnson**

A four-dimensional model of purpose

Over many years, I have observed the journeys of countless purpose seekers and listened to the stories of their process. Gradually, this collection of observations started to crystallize in my mind and take shape as a purpose flow-diagram that describes a cyclical interplay of elements.

Before I describe my purpose flow model, I want to honor its thought lineage. My model is built atop the foundation of a four-part Venn diagram of purpose created by Anais Bock in 2012. Her model went viral and it continues to circulate widely today. You have probably seen some version of this diagram. In some variations, the central section or solution set of the four-part figure is labeled as *ikigai* — the Japanese word meaning "reason for being." (For more on the history of this term, see the bonus content: "The Cultural Appropriation of Ikigai.")

This Venn diagram has shaped the view of purpose as an alchemical mix of four main ingredients. It shows purpose located at the intersection of four things:

1. What you're good at
2. What you love to do
3. What the world needs
4. What you get paid for

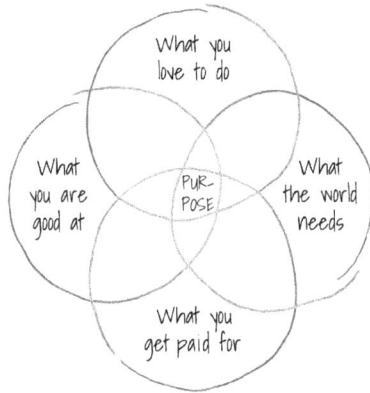

When I had the opportunity to speak with Anais about her creation, she shared with me her rationale for adding the fourth dimension: "What you get paid for."

When I created the four-part purpose diagram, I was modifying an earlier version made by a primary school teacher, Ms. Dorothy. It had the three overlapping circles of what you love, what you're good at, and what the world needs. I added the fourth one: what you get paid for. I found that the way we were talking about purpose, it was always a purely feminine conversation. Either we were talking about love and changing the world, or we were talking structures, and money, and this is how the world works. They were two separate conversations.

I didn't like that there was this divide where the masculine world is the real stuff and the feminine world is the fluffy stuff. It perpetuates an idea that purpose work is dream work. Maybe purpose is what gets you started on a path. But the problem with this divide is that when it's time to actually bring your purpose work into reality, you find out it doesn't work anymore. That's when you are confronted with the harsh reality that we all need to survive with money. And succeeding in that harsh reality requires a scarcity mindset, strategy, and competition. My creation of that four-part purpose diagram was my way of saying that we need to have a balance. We need to integrate both masculine and feminine aspects when pursuing purpose work. Seeing how these two aspects can co-exist in balance is a major theme of my work. I am a bridge worker.

The idea is that by identifying the work roles, functions, or activities that fit into those four circles and then looking for the area where they overlap, the solution set will reveal your life purpose. I do believe that the four categories in this diagram are foundational to understanding purpose as a complex composite of several different dimensions of work-life. Yet, while coaching clients using this model, these four core concepts began to morph and move before my eyes, and I observed a more dynamic version of purpose work emerging.

I found myself wondering: How might we expand upon this static four-part purpose model and make it come alive? How might we make purpose into something more real and more relevant for the world we live in today?

Introducing a new paradigm of purpose

We can illustrate the dynamic nature of regenerative purpose by turning the four-part Venn diagram into a four-part flow diagram. The four overlapping circles become one continuous, virtuous cycle. Purpose is not the undiscovered answer to a riddle; it is not that mythical space in the middle. No, regenerative purpose is an omnipresent aspect of human nature. We can modify the saying, "I think therefore I am," to be, "I exist therefore purpose exists." Purpose is not something to seek; it exists here and now. We can give up the role of seeker and drop the quest for purpose. The new paradigm of purpose invites us to embody the dancer; to allow ourselves to move with the flow of nature that surrounds us and inhabits us.

How regenerative purpose flows

We start to see that purpose is not a thing for us to discover; not a place for us to arrive at. It is a way that we choose to live. Purpose may offer perspective on *why* we do what we do. It may even provide insight into *how* we do it. Yet, ultimately, purpose is a never-ending process of evolution. Following the purpose path is edge-finding, invigorating, and deliciously unpredictable. In the new paradigm of purpose, purpose is no longer the solution to a Venn diagram. Purpose is now the inquiry that sparks a lifelong exploration.

Two elements in conversation

Here is my audacious claim: In walking our purpose path, there is no seeking needed; there is no figuring out required. We do not need to find or forge a way to get to our purpose. Purpose is a natural, impersonal process. We simply get out of the way and let purpose take its course through us.

The category formerly known as "what you're good at" becomes the individual element. It is totality of everything that makes us who we are. It is our unique expression of humanity.

The category formerly known as "what the world needs" becomes the collective element. It includes the variety and vastness of everything that we perceive and experience in the wider world, no matter whether it is beautiful or maddening, inspiring or devastating. This is the worldview we have, which is colored by our specific sensitivities.

The individual and collective elements set up a dyad for dialogue. We are both a person *in the world*, and at the same time, a part *of the world*, engaging in a dynamic shared reality. The individual and collective elements are participants in a conversation, and they are constantly co-evolving. We will explore these elements more in the next chapter.

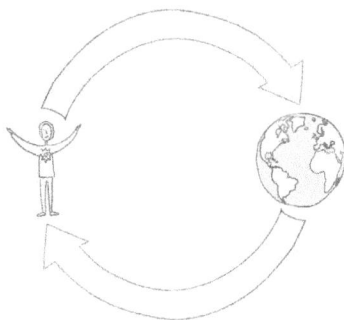

Two movements in balance

In the new paradigm of purpose, there is nowhere we need to go. What matters is that we move with intention wherever we are right now. The way we choose to move — in every "here" and in every "now" — is what fosters a sustainable, mutually nourishing exchange between us and the world.

In the purpose flow diagram, the category formerly known as "what you love to do" becomes a movement of giving (represented by the top arrow moving from left to right). This is energy moving from the individual to the collective. It is the expression of love. When this is free to move, we feel the flow of creativity. Then the category formerly known as "what you get paid for" becomes a movement of receiving (represented by the bottom arrow moving from right to left). This is energy coming from the world to support and guide the individual. When this is free to move, we tap into the flow of abundance. In this circle, we see how our energy moves out into the world and then comes back around, returning to us. The completion of the cycle is what makes purpose sustainable.

Purpose as a force of nature

In the old-school model of purpose, we find purpose by solving for the intersection of four static categories. This outdated view treats humans as independent actors focused on their personal projects of empire-building. In the new paradigm, we experience purpose by cultivating inner qualities that support our participation in a co-creative conversation with a shared, dynamic reality. As we step into this as the new normal, humans become interdependent elements, serving as vehicles for the collective force of planetary movement-making.

With regenerative purpose, we animate the four static categories that were once used to locate our purpose in the middle of the Venn diagram. In the new model, these four dimensions now create a dynamic flow cycle, made up of two elements in a dyad (individual and collective), engaged in two balanced, reciprocal movements (giving and receiving).

This flow cycle reveals purpose as a force of nature. It is a full circle, a full cycle. When giving and receiving are balanced, we create a circular exchange of energy between the individual and the collective. The movement of the flow cycle represents how we are always responding to and receiving from the world, repeatedly, and simultaneously.

With this perspective, we no longer have to go on a heroic journey to answer the question, "What is your purpose?" The purpose path is revealed as the humbling process of making ourselves more available to answer to life. Instead of trying to pursue purpose, our work becomes continuously removing obstacles that are blocking the natural flow of purpose.

Cultivating purpose flow

If we can accept that the work of purpose will never be finished, then how do we get started? How do we unleash the flow of purpose in our lives? In my own life and in my work with clients, I have seen purpose enlivened by the development of four core purpose qualities. I see these as the essence qualities underlying the four common themes in how we experience purpose — the same themes that were described in my interviews.

In other words, we step back and observe, how am I being and what am I doing when I feel like I am on purpose? The inquiry that arises then is: What are the inner qualities that I can intentionally cultivate within myself to welcome that experience into my life more and more?

The four core purpose qualities are Authenticity, Attunement, Responsiveness, and Receptivity. Our most unique, valuable gifts are effortlessly revealed when we cultivate Authenticity. Our intelligent sensitivity to how we can best serve others arises when we cultivate Attunement. Creative expression is enlivened when we cultivate Responsiveness. Abundance consciousness expands when we cultivate Receptivity. When I am in the flow of regenerative purpose, I am authentic; I am attuned; I am responding; and I am receiving.

In the new paradigm, purpose is not a problem that you solve once and then you're done. We align, we fall away, and we re-align, again and again. As we cultivate the four core purpose qualities within ourselves through practice, we start to experience purpose more frequently and more consistently. But it's not a permanent state. It requires discipline of the mind and devotion of the heart to stay steady in this — and to gently keep bringing ourselves back when we falter or forget.

We activate attraction between the individual and collective elements — the positive and negative poles — by cultivating the qualities of being: Authenticity and Attunement. These "being qualities" help us open up clear channels of communication between us and the world. We expand the energy that is exchanged in this conversation by cultivating the qualities of doing: Responsiveness and Receptivity. These "doing qualities" help facilitate the flow of giving and receiving by guiding how we choose to move in the world. What we experience when we embody the four core purpose qualities is *regenerative purpose*.

Regenerative purpose requires balance in many dimensions: a balance of being and doing; a balance of giving and receiving; a balance of creative inspiration and practical foundation; a balance of focused devotion and surrendered availability. It is holding clear intention without attachment to outcome. It is having openness with healthy boundaries. It is welcoming both creation and destruction. Without the burdens we carry from conditioning, the cycle of purpose becomes effortless. There is an ease in giving and receiving. Creativity and abundance feel expansive. The attraction between the positive and negative poles, along with the balanced movements of giving and receiving, are fundamental to the dynamic nature of purpose. The yin and yang, the sky and ground, the push and pull, the coming and going — these keep the wheel of life turning. In this way, the purpose cycle is infinitely regenerative.

If the question, "What is your purpose?" feels too vast, then you can release the compulsion to answer it. "How do you want to live?" might be a more useful question to consider instead. This question opens up a more manageable inquiry, and the insights that it brings can be tested out in real life right away. With regenerative purpose, you do not need to have a statement to summarize your reason for being. We can be freed from purpose as a question we have to answer. It feels more spacious to treat purpose as a conversation we choose to enter.

CHAPTER 3

The Dynamic Elements of Purpose Flow

To me it's not a negative thing to know that there will be great changes. It's evolution. Over time, nothing stays the same. It's never the end. There is no end to life.
— **Floyd (Red Crow) Westerman**

To see how regenerative purpose works, we start by taking a closer look at the two elements and the two movements that make up the purpose flow model. Let's redefine them and see how they are different from the static categories of the classic four-part Venn diagram. When we are working with the dynamic flow of purpose, there are subtle but significant distinctions in how we view these dimensions.

"What you are good at" becomes Genius In Fluid Truth (GIFT)

In the first dimension, we transform the category of "what you are good at" into the individual element, which is now more broadly referred to as Genius In Fluid Truth (GIFT). Genius points to the exceptional powers that are uniquely ours to harness and hold as individuals. The fluid expression of our specific superpowers emerges in the present moment when supported by the field of truth.

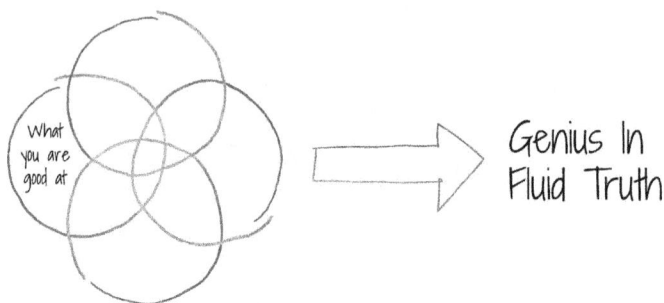

What
you are
good at

Genius In
Fluid Truth

When we think of our gifts, what usually comes to mind are things that we are good at — our skills and talents. These could be abilities awarded by genetic lottery or hard-won achievements of study and training. Either way, we typically view gifts as *things we do well.* While our skills and talents are part of our offering, there's more to it than that. A broader definition of gifts is the sum of *everything we are given in life.*

Our Genius In Fluid Truth (GIFT) includes all of the raw materials that we have to work with as we create our lives. They are the basic ingredients stocked in our purpose-making pantry. Some are innate, while others are imprinted by life experiences. Some are developed with effort, while others are rather random. And the unique collection of assets we hold is ever-evolving and ever-expanding throughout our lives.

This personal basket of blessings can appear bountiful, or it can be largely buried. To reveal their full potential, gifts must not only be given; they must also be recognized, owned, wielded, and nurtured. The ingredients that we have can do us little good if they are left sitting on the pantry shelf. We can intentionally bring forth more Genius In Fluid Truth by increasing awareness and activation of these raw materials.

Capability gifts

The classic definition of gifts as "what you are good at" falls into the bucket that I call capability gifts. These are potentials within us that are relatively well-developed. They are usually obvious to us and already observable in our current actions and interactions with the world. For the most part, they are also recognized and reinforced by those around us.

Examples of capability gifts include:

- Knowing how to make the perfect espresso macchiato
- Having two decades of experience as a marine biologist
- Speaking fluent Sarsi (a rare Navajo language)
- Being qualified to facilitate a design thinking process
- Understanding the medicinal properties of local plant life

Capacity gifts

It is helpful to take inventory of what we are good at; to assess and acknowledge all the things we do well. Then we can widen the scope of our viewfinder, by seeing the large collection of potentials that make up our capacity gifts. Some of our personal potential is already apparent, or more developed. Some of our personal potential is latent, or less developed. By including all of the untapped potential that is at rest within us, we expand our notion of gifts. We start to see gifts not just as a basket of abilities, but more fully as a container of possibilities.

The less-developed potentials within us are capacities. They are not fully in our awareness because they are hidden under the surface. They are not fully integrated in our current actions. They are not on display for others to witness. A capacity is simply a dormant capability. It already exists, but it has not yet been recognized, owned, and nurtured to its full potential.

For example, I grew up in a Chinese-speaking household. In the first few years of my life, before going to public school kindergarten in the United States, I was immersed in the sounds of the Chinese language in my home environment. I do speak and understand some Chinese, but I am not proficient. However, my subconscious has taken in many specific sounds or phonemes required for near-native pronunciation of Chinese. If I were to invest in taking Chinese language classes, I would naturally have a learning advantage over other people who were not exposed to the sounds of this language in their early life. This is a capacity of mine, which remains undeveloped.

Examples of capacity gifts include:

- Learning dance moves and sequences quickly
- Having an aptitude for mechanical things
- Remembering names of new people with ease
- Being a naturally articulate public speaker
- Having a refined palate for tasting food

A lot of self-help culture likes to emphasize untapped potential. But the flip side of this is recognizing the capacities that we do *not* have. It means acknowledging when there are functions better served by someone else, or roles better filled by others. Our undeveloped capacities are unseen, but they are not infinite. Anyone can learn to play guitar if they apply time and effort to the development of that skill, but not everyone can learn to play like Jimi Hendrix. We each have certain advantages or disadvantages when it comes to acquiring different abilities. This is part of what makes us unique. Our capacities set us apart from others who are less equipped or less inclined to develop the same skills and talents.

Characteristic gifts

With our work ethic bias, we tend to recognize more of the gifts that have been earned. Capabilities and capacities are given to us, but they are not entirely free. These gifts also require focus and intention in order to be fully realized. We do things to nurture and develop these gifts. Earned gifts can be attributed to our education, our training, or our experience. We may feel deserving of these gifts — or even entitled to them — due to personal merit or effort invested.

Unearned gifts introduce another dimension of what we are given — and these blessings are often overlooked. To embrace and exercise our full potential, it's important to include unearned gifts in our awareness too.

Characteristics are unearned gifts. They are given to us by accident of birth. Those gifts can include our skin color, gender, nationality, native language, physical features, or family of origin. We all have certain aspects of our biological, cultural, and contextual makeup that can give us advantages or opportunities.

Examples of characteristic gifts include:

- Enjoying perfect 20/20 vision in both eyes
- Holding a United States passport
- Presenting or passing as racially white
- Being born into a wealthy family
- Growing up as a native English speaker

Characteristic gifts are easy to miss. Things that are notable to others don't even register on our radar, because we simply don't know life without them; they are part of our background. We were "born this way." These gifts are invisible to us because we take them for granted. Yet it's important to remember the characteristic gifts that have been given to us.

Even when we are aware of our characteristic gifts, we often look the other way. Since unearned gifts are not rubber-stamped by the rule of meritocracy, we turn a blind eye to them by reflex. For example, the gifts associated with a specific gender or race can be tough to acknowledge. It's easier to declare that equality has been accomplished or pretend that we are color-blind. However, systemic biases are baked into our current reality. If we are born with advantages in an unjust society, we have two options: We can either own our platform of privilege and intentionally use it to lift up others who are less visible and less able, or we can deny and dismiss our advantage.

In disowning our characteristic gifts, we miss the chance to wield their power to consciously serve. If we do not confront the repressed shame and guilt that we carry as the bearers of these unearned gifts, we will be blocked from effectively using them to benefit the greater good.

Circumstance gifts

Circumstances are another type of unearned gift. These unearned gifts include the events that happen to us or through us or around us. Our circumstances give us valuable perspectives and platforms. They embed value from experience.

Negative circumstances are usually seen as obstacles to overcome. Yet these challenges can also help us stand out from the crowd because they color our lives. As we live through and integrate our hardships over time, they become assets. We are each the sole bearer and bringer of lessons from our personal experience. Our life story uniquely qualifies us to connect with, speak to, and work with certain others — those with a similar story, on a similar path. We have embodied knowledge that cannot be trained or transmitted from a textbook. Deep trust is fostered when we recognize another human being who knows our journey intimately from their own lived experience. This kind of resonance cannot be manufactured.

Positive circumstances offer blessings, as long as we can acknowledge the advantages they give us. Much like with the privileges afforded by our characteristic gifts, we may shy away from fully owning our positive circumstances, out of guilt or shame. When we find ourselves in the throes of good fortune, the difference between showing up and showing off is an orientation of service.

Examples of circumstance gifts include:

- Enduring personal or business bankruptcy
- Inheriting a valuable piece of property
- Leaving a domestic abuse situation
- Winning a million dollars in the lottery
- Conceiving via in-vitro fertilization

What we are good at is a part of our love offering to the world — but it is only a part. We need to zoom out to see the whole picture. Beyond what we are good at, we also have capacities that we can nurture and develop. We are also born with a set of unique characteristics that may give us some advantages. And we are blessed with the experiences created by our individual circumstances. As we develop in Authenticity, we recognize and own the full spectrum of assets that we are given. Then we can start to make better use of the raw materials that we have available to us.

"What the world needs" becomes Personally Activating INformation (PAIN)

In new-paradigm purpose, the category of "what the world needs" becomes the collective element in the conversation. In the regenerative purpose flow cycle, this element is now labeled as Personally Activating INformation (PAIN). In a way, this collective element is also personal, because it is an individual-specific sensitivity to what is happening in the world. It is how we each hear the call of the collective. It is the receipt of *information* from our environment. It is *activating* because it focuses attention and generates intention. It is *personal*, because without applying our individual sensitivity filter, the signals that come to us are only input not impetus. A signal may not garner any attention from one person, while being extremely galvanizing for another. Even though the size of an object in the mirror can be measured on an absolute scale, the way that it appears to our individual perception is far from universal.

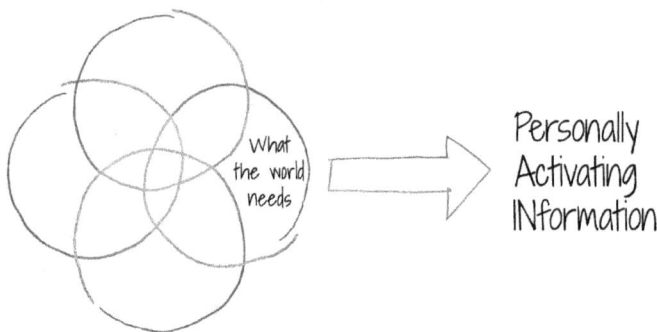

What the world needs → Personally Activating INformation

Projection of what the world needs

In modern life, we receive a non-stop stream of data: email requests, news stories, text messages, buying signals, and personal feedback from our environment. There's a flood of information entering our field of awareness from everywhere, all the time. The sheer volume of signals that we are constantly bombarded with can make it challenging to pick up on the most important ones.

It is true that we face many challenges in our world today. Yet when we ask ourselves what the world needs, we will necessarily come up with an answer that is a product of thinking. We must create a mental projection to answer this question. We have to perform some mental gymnastics to manufacture an idea of what the world needs. We have to imagine something that needs to be fixed or solved or helped or healed.

When we set out on our purpose journey by asking what the world needs, our perception can easily be hijacked or distorted. Unchecked, the ideas we come up with about "what the world needs" can gradually solidify into *ideals*. When we are too focused on ideals, it can make us impenetrable to real, live information that is available to us from moment to moment. We separate ourselves from the dynamic nature of reality by constructing — and then dwelling in — our ideals. The world does not revolve around us; the world evolves around us.

When we are connected to our deepest core, we can see that our concept of "what the world needs" is actually a big screen reflection of the Personally Activating INformation (PAIN) that registers in our own systems as we move around in the world.

To stay in true contact with the ongoing shifts in our outer reality, we need to be in constant contact with our inner selves.

When we open to receive the information that comes from feeling into those sensitive places, we start to notice where we are most called to serve.

The concept of "what the world needs" is impossibly vast. It is also incredibly vague. For the sake of purpose, the thoughts, feelings, and sensations that we experience in interaction with the world are only useful if they help us identify aligned actions. Our PAIN points us to the specific actions that we are uniquely wired for, to make the biggest impact.

Sensing the world by seeing within

The opportunity lies in becoming less concerned with what we *think* the world needs and instead more focused on filtering and interpreting the information that we are always receiving. With this orientation, PAIN becomes a signpost for us, a marker that guides us on our way. What is important here is selectively listening with conscious intention.

The information that is relevant to us comes through when we tune into Personally Activating INformation. It's less about thinking, and more about feeling and sensing. We notice how we are affected by different situations, and observe how we are touched by different stories. We tune into how we are, when we are connected with the world. It is about being present in a relational field with reality and deepening it with awareness.

The PAIN sensations we experience can feel overwhelming when we are out of balance. For example, when we are taking care of others too much — and not taking care of ourselves enough — the pain we feel can be slightly irritating at best, or completely paralyzing at worst. On the other hand, PAIN can provide focus for us if we intentionally access its intelligence from a place of balance.

Experience as focus and fuel

We can drop the idea of "what the world needs." This dimension of purpose is limiting if we treat it as a belief about what reality demands from us. This is what shifts in the new paradigm of purpose. We are not asserting some universal, objective truth *about* the world. Instead we are acknowledging our individual, subjective experience *in* the world. We notice our own state in the face of certain circumstances, situations, or structures. Neatly folded within that noticing, there is valuable data to help us find our place in the world.

Let's take practicing palliative care physician Jessica Montalvo, as an example. Dr. Montalvo is establishing her own private practice in functional medicine. Due to some family misfortune, she became a financial steward for her parents at a relatively young age. Recently, her father had a medical event that compromised his ability to live independently, which led to her taking on the responsibility of 24-hour care for him. She shared how this personal experience has contributed to her motivation to change the trajectory of her work-life.

> *What is happening in the [US] healthcare system is nuts. The way our healthcare dollars are spent is ridiculous. Instead of taking care of people at home, teaching them basic skills and providing them with tools to have a healthy lifestyle, we let them get really sick — to the point where they have to go to the hospital — and then we throw all these expensive treatments at them that aren't actually going to*

make them better. This makes me so mad. Of course, what
happened with my parents lights a fire under me. I want to
prevent this from happening to other families. If medicine
was focused on teaching people how to design their lives for
optimal health, instead of treating people when they are
already deteriorating, we would have much better outcomes
at a much lower cost.

Instead of looking outside to see what needs fixing, let's start by looking within to see what touches us deeply and move from there. When we allow our sensitivity to guide us, then we are not driven by the idea of being a helper or savior. By tuning in to Personally Activating INformation (PAIN), we become humbly engaged in our own healing and growth. And we heal the world by healing ourselves. Helping the world becomes a natural byproduct of our personal evolutionary process.

The activation of information

PAIN includes, but is not limited to, the pain that causes us to say "ouch." Of course, there are many scenarios in life that lead us to experience hurt or suffering. But there is something more primary than that: the thing that enters our nervous system before the brain interprets it to generate an "ouch" response. It is the signal that comes through when a stimulus in our surroundings causes a strong sensation or makes a memorable impression. We have a certain experience and it strikes us in such a way that we suddenly sit up and take note of it. We find ourselves in a specific situation and it rubs us in a place where we are especially sensitive.

Feminist marketing coach Kelly Diels says: "Feelings are

clues, not codes. They don't contain all the information; they're a prompt to look for more information." What she points out here can be applied to PAIN when we understand it as Personally Activating INformation. It does not hand us the whole story from cover to cover. This kind of PAIN acts more like a highlighter; it marks a particular passage in the book. It draws attention to an intriguing insight that you want to remember, or a place of interest where you want to dig deeper.

Personally Activating INformation creates a point of focus but it does not dictate a specific response. The action emerges in the interplay of external information we are sensitive to and internal resources we have access to.

For example, if you are a deejay, you might feel the dynamics in a room and have a "spidey sense" about what music track will bring a group of people to ecstasy. If you are a doula, you might listen to the breathing pattern of a birthing mother and intuitively know which position will ease her labor. If you are an interrogation specialist, you might read body language and have a hunch about the perfect next question to ask. It is the interaction of Personally Activating INformation and the individual's authentic gift that allows purpose to unfold.

Cry me a river... of glitter

I started a small online business in 2016, which was sparked by Personally Activating INformation.

> *I was at a dance party on a remote beach in Thailand. There were about a hundred people at this happy hippie fest. We were dancing, singing, and overflowing with love, and joy, and glitter. Everyone was having an amazing time, high*

on life and other things.

It was a hot day. To cool off, I went to the ocean with a few friends. We were giddy with gratitude, feeling free and blessed. We were swimming... jumping... splashing... We were like children discovering the ocean for the first time.

At one point, I looked down at the turquoise waters surrounding me. I saw a flotilla of golden sparkles dancing in the sunlight on the surface of the water and I thought, "how beautiful."

A split second later, a lightning bolt of awareness hit me. I realized with a shock, "Oh shit. That glitter is plastic. And it's in the ocean. That's not beautiful. That's tragic."

Suddenly, tears were streaming down my face. I crawled out of the water sobbing, and feeling nauseous with guilt over the price that Mother Nature would have to pay for our afternoon of fun. My biodegradable glitter business Glitterevolution was conceived in that moment.

I had never been a festival kid who spent summers covered head to toe in glitter. I had used conventional glitter sparingly and only occasionally before that day. I had never entertained ambitions of having an online business. I had never even considered it. Yet I never questioned that this is what I needed to do. After crying on the beach that day, my heart was on fire.

Within a few months, I launched my biodegradable glitter business. That sudden moment of insight on the beach had made such a strong impression on me; it became the catalyst that powered me through months of work. There was research, planning, organizing, and infrastructure building to do. The activation energy from that afternoon is what fueled me as I played with different formulas, tested packaging, designed a logo, and built a website.

This business provides a service to others. At the same time, it is a solution to my own problem. It resolves an inner conflict that I experienced as a split within myself. I want to enjoy the childlike playfulness and shining self-expression that glitter represents. I also want to embody the mature adult who accepts stewardship of the Earth as a serious responsibility. The message I am broadcasting with this business is the message that I longed to hear: You don't have to give up your enjoyment of life to be a conscious caretaker of the planet.

The new definition of this dimension of purpose calls us to look beyond "what [we think] the world needs." Instead of enlisting the mind to create projections of the needs of the world, we turn inward. We tune into what touches our hearts and listen to the deep wisdom that lies in our body intelligence. When we start to notice what we are sensitive to as we move around the world, the signal of our calling starts to come through more clearly.

"What you love to do" becomes Creative Flow

In the new paradigm of purpose, the category of "what you love to do" becomes movement in the direction of giving, from the individual to the collective. It is the embodied experience of Creative Flow. This flow is unleashed when we are aligned in giving. It is the expression of love from each of us to the world.

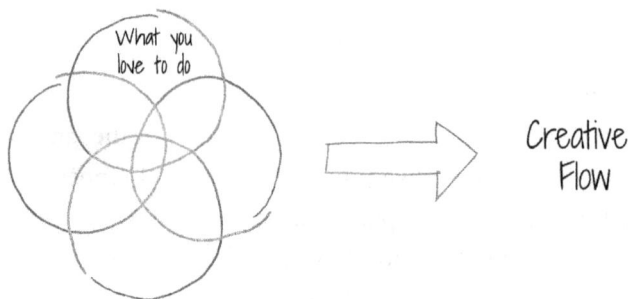

What you love to do

Creative Flow

Choosing pleasure over pressure

The inclusion of "what we love to do" in the four-part purpose diagram represents a necessary step in the evolution of purpose. It challenges the Protestant work ethic that we have inherited in the Western world. As my linguist friend Kim explained to me, "In Protestantism, the only job man has on Earth is to serve God, and life on Earth was seen as suffering. Everything was predetermined by God and He chose the best and most virtuous of us for the hardest work. Hence, suffering for God, bearing hardships and working like a dog, were seen as a sign of being a 'chosen one' to enter into the realm of Heaven. The Industrial Revolution deconsecrated these norms and institutionalized them in new ways. Nowadays it is even worse, we don't even believe in the reward of heaven anymore, yet still we enslave ourselves to the system!"

The legacy of Protestantism comes with certain beliefs as byproducts: work is demanding; work is depleting; when we work, we earn esteem for enduring hardship. These concepts were further codified in the industrial economy, where the workforce was trained to react to external pressure so they could easily be directed, managed, and motivated by their bosses. To transition out of this hierarchy reality, we need to learn to follow the guidance system of personal pleasure. The pleasure principle is an antidote to seeking suffering as a fool's prize.

How does our relationship with work change as we retire from our role in the old-paradigm power dynamic? Silent, long-forgotten parts of us start to speak out. We become intimate with our deepest truth. We say no to pressure more often. We say yes to pleasure more. We see how we can stand up for the world we want to see. We become emboldened to choose the kind of work we want to do. We begin to prioritize purpose with courage and conviction.

When it comes to matters of pleasure, the body knows best. When we decide what to do by default, we usually rely on our understanding of roles and obligations — all constructs held in the mind. However, we need to connect with our body intelligence. It sometimes feels uncomfortable to follow the direction of our own desires instead of meeting others' expectations. But if we can endure this discomfort, we can start to listen to our own internal guidance system, instead of complying with external forces. Shifting our orientation from pressure to pleasure helps us relocate the locus of control. We move from external authority to inner authority — and reclaim our autonomy. We no longer need to mold our behavior to feed a system. We no longer need to betray ourselves to conform to someone else's plans. From that place of freedom, service work pours forth as the natural byproduct of self-love.

The path beyond pleasure

Focusing on pleasure is a good way to check in with our inner voice, since falling in line with existing power structures often feels so natural that we don't even notice that we're doing it. Whether it's saying "yes" to sex on the third date or saying "yes" to working all weekend to meet a deadline, we are all conditioned to subvert our individual will to the demands of the dominant culture. The idea that work can be enjoyable can help us break the habit of mindlessly sacrificing ourselves on the altar of work. This is the deconditioning power of self-help memes that cheer for us to "follow our bliss" — yet when we take a step back, we can see there is something these memes miss.

Visual artist and author Elle Luna described the tension between conditioned obligations and heart-led convictions in *The Crossroads of Should and Must.* But traveling from *should* to *must* is not always so straightforward. For me personally, it was a gradual transition. The classic four-part purpose Venn diagram model highlights "what we love to do" as a key part of the purpose mix. Indeed, our passions and pleasures can guide us through a gentler transition between *should* and *must.* Following our bliss brings us to an important waypoint on the purpose path. In other words, "what we love to do" is a layover on a longer journey: a place that many of us pass through after departing from *should,* before arriving at *must.*

As we discard the oppressive myth of self-sacrifice, the pleasure principle orients us towards enjoying work. With this first frame shift, we release ourselves from the pressure cooker of old power structures. Then, once we have learned to stop forgoing self-love for the sake of our work, we find space to step up again. This second frame shift moves us past the playground of hedonic pursuits into the realm of higher purpose.

Pressure dictates what we *should* do. Pleasure guides us to what we *like (or love)* to do. Purpose reveals what we *must* do.

Clinical sexologist Martha Lee spoke about her experience of this compelling sense of *must* — the choiceless choice.

> *Whether you call it your life purpose or your mission or your calling, it is something much deeper. It's something that you feel you were put on Earth to do and you have to do it, no matter what. And this thing that you want to do, well actually, you don't want to do it. You don't want to do it because it's hard. But you just know you have to do it. It scares you and it makes you excited at the same time. It puts you on that edge of fear and excitement. It's not easy but you do it anyway. You have no choice.*

Purpose work is not always pleasurable. Sometimes, it's not even pleasant. If we expect it to be a ticket to perpetual bliss, we will be disappointed. Purpose requires devotion to something beyond our personal preferences and concerns. Mark Manson challenges us to consider: "What's your favorite flavor of shit sandwich? Everything sucks, some of the time. If you love and want something enough — whatever it is — then you don't really mind eating the shit sandwich that comes with it." No matter how beautiful, inspiring, and exciting our purpose work seems during the honeymoon phase, some unpleasant aspects will arise at some point. We just have to choose the kind of shit sandwich we are willing to eat.

To put it simply, purpose work is not what we love to do; purpose work is what we do from love.

What we do from love

Last year, I hosted a booth at a music festival to share and sell my plant-based biodegradable glitter. I wanted to offer an eco-friendly alternative to the polyester glitter that is everywhere at these kinds of gatherings, with unaware festival goers leaving a trail of microplastic pollution in their sparkly wake.

My team was stationed in a poorly trafficked area of the festival grounds. The people who happened to stumble upon our booth were not interested in saving the Earth. The festival coordinators were disorganized and stressed out. The people around me were struggling with logistical challenges and complaining loudly. I did not enjoy the music. The food was awful and expensive. I was not loving my work.

The experience was draining to me, physically, emotionally, and financially. I had a terrible time. Yet the opportunity was absolutely aligned from the perspective of purpose.

In accepting the invitation to participate, I stubbornly refused to hand over my biodegradable glitter to the festival organizers' vending team. I was adamant that I did not want them to offer it for sale at the glitter station where they were decorating festival-goers with conventional polyester glitter. I stood firm in my view that doing so would pollute the purity of my message. This meant that I would accept fewer sales while putting in more effort to manage a separate booth. The organizers were fairly perplexed by my choice, but for me, it was not about maximizing profit for minimal effort. It was about carrying a message, raising awareness, and staying in integrity.

Remembering my "why" helped me stay centered. I was there to educate festival-goers about the microplastic pollution problem of conventional glitter. I was there to offer a biodegradable option. I was there to invite questions about the origin and destination of all the things we buy, use, consume, and throw away. In these ways, the event was a huge success.

There are a few turns in this path — from pressure to pleasure to purpose. Unburdened from performance pressure, we start to find pleasure in what we do. Then once we are standing firm in the strength of our sovereign will, we can see beyond the pursuit of fleeting gratification. From there, we touch a more nourishing, soul-level satisfaction that takes us way beyond the self-indulgent enjoyment of the current moment. This alignment with purpose resonates on a much deeper level. It brings us an enduring, existential sort of joy that comes from the full expression of our love in this lifetime. As poet Khalil Gibran says, "Work is love made visible."

Experiencing the movement of Creative Flow requires that we first free ourselves from the binds of external demands, and then, from ego-centric desires. The creative energy that is available in purpose work includes and expands beyond the creativity that we associate with artistic expression in painting, music, or dance. Here, we are speaking about the art of channeling the creative force that is inherent in life. Creation is what naturally arises in any domain where we respond from presence, rather than reacting from a pre-installed program. Moving from loving presence is what unlocks Creative Flow.

"What you get paid for" becomes Abundance Flow

In the purpose flow model, the category of "what you get paid for" becomes a movement of energy from the collective back to the individual. Abundance Flow is what we experience when we are aligned in the direction of receiving. It is the movement of love returning from the world to each of us.

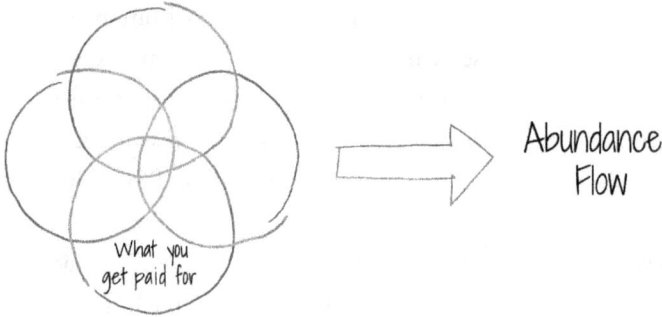

The non-duality of money and meaning

The idea of "what you love to do" helped us get over the idea that work should require suffering. Similarly, the inclusion of "what you get paid for" in the four-part purpose diagram was also a necessary step in the evolution of purpose.

Somewhere along the line, we bought into the belief that purpose is extracurricular. We are misguided in believing it is something we indulge in only after our day job is done. First, we make sure we get paid, then we can play with purpose in the time that is left over. This reinforces the false duality between practical concerns and purposeful creation.

Service does not necessarily mean sacrifice. Including the category of "what you get paid for" in the purpose diagram posed an important challenge to outmoded thinking that held cause-related work as charity work — or even, what was once condescendingly called "women's work." Historically, there was this idea that the work we do for money is *over here* and the work we do for meaning is *over there*. With Anais Bock's addition of "what you get paid for" into the purpose diagram, we stopped buying into the separation of money and meaning.

The separation of money and meaning prevents us from getting paid fairly for purpose work. We cannot flourish when we block financial support. We might resist support because we don't feel we deserve to receive money for our work. Or, we might refuse support because we have a morally superior self-image that relies on us not caring about money. Indeed, many heart-led entrepreneurs have confided in me that they feel getting paid taints the purity of their purpose. It's true that money can be corrupting. Yet, not allowing money to come in is completely crippling. In business, we talk about minimum requirements for maintaining a physical presence as "keeping the lights on and doors open." Similarly, we have to meet basic needs for money in our purpose work — to keep our personal Light on, and our hearts open.

Abundance Flow is, in part, about welcoming financial support. Including "what you get paid for" as a dimension of purpose is a declaration of integration. It loudly announces that we are ready for purpose work to be fully woven into the fabric of our lives. We are ready to be rewarded — and not sacrificed — on the purpose path. We know now that money is not the purpose. Yet we must remember that money acts as fuel for our purpose. Money is the lifeblood that allows the purpose-expressing organism to survive in the physical dimension.

Getting paid what you're worth

Under the banner of women's financial liberation "getting paid what you're worth" has become a popular empowerment mantra. Fair pay is surely an important pillar in the ongoing fight for equality. Women are still chronically underpaid compared to their male counterparts at the office. We generally fail to recognize and compensate women for their work in the home. Yet centering so much around "getting paid" in our discussions of self-worth is somewhat misguided.

Kelly Diels helps explain what is problematic about it:

I have an itchiness around the exhortation for us to "get paid what you're worth." I recognize and celebrate what we're trying to do with that rally cry, how we're trying to close the wage gap, how we're trying to stop cosigning our own financial marginalization. Let's keep doing that. And. But. As humans, we are irreplaceable. As culture makers and cultural workers, our worth is more than rubies and pearls and six figure incomes or seven figure launches. Our worth and the value we create will ALWAYS outstrip our monetary compensation. You're deserving of rights and resources just because you are here and you were born — and what a gift to all of us that you were. Your value can never be matched by something as generic and replicable as money. So please inhabit your irreplaceability AND honor your lineage and your work to ask and negotiate for what you need and want to thrive.

What we get paid is determined in the interplay of two things: first, the sense of self-worth we hold within ourselves, and second, what is currently valued in the cultural and economic system that we swim in. As purpose pioneers, we will find ourselves bridging a gap. There will be a moment when we need to stand firm in our conviction in what we personally value, while staring down conflict and confusion about what society collectively values. Often, the things we value as purpose leaders are not yet valued by the majority of people on the planet.

In other cases, people may say they value something, but it is not evident in the way they express and exchange value. We say that we value our health, but we continue to stock our cabinets with sugar-laden snacks. We say that we value intimate, in-person connection, but we spend hours mindlessly scrolling through social media. We say that we value nurses, teachers, artists, and activists, but with our entertainment habits, we continue to feed the advertising dollars that inflate the salaries of movie stars and professional athletes.

At the level of individual exchange, our charge is to find the right match. If we can decouple our sense of self-worth from a dollar figure, then we can see that value is subjective. Whether something is expensive or inexpensive is not absolute. What is considered a bargain for one person is a clear extravagance for another. What others value depends on their money story, their resources, their needs, and their priorities. Instead of setting prices that are pinned to a perception of self-worth, we need to focus on creating exchanges that are positive for both parties.

Ever-present enoughness

Not having enough financial support to power our purpose can put us in survival mode. Of course, the contraction, tension, stress, and anxiety that come with that feeling of scarcity are not conducive to creation. You might think that this would be more problematic for those who are less resourced, but Lynne Twist debunks this myth around scarcity in her book, *The Soul of Money*. She looked at money beliefs shared across resource-rich and resource-poor members of society. What she found was that the experience of never having enough and always needing more is common across the political, economic, and cultural spectrum. It doesn't matter whether we are rich or poor, we all suffer from scarcity. This constant feeling of lack is what drives our modern, capitalist oligarchy. It keeps our energy tied up in the hamster wheel of consumption rather than invested in nourishing connection and creation.

This loop of not-enoughness can be a dangerous trap. It seems inescapable because a lack mindset is both self-fulfilling and self-perpetuating. We get caught up in a crazy-making storm of competing, hustling, and scrambling to accumulate wealth. We end up in a race to secure more for ourselves. We forget that resources are actually "we"-sources and we get fixated on resource acquisition for one instead of resource access for all.

The paradox is that while fear and scarcity are part of our cultural conditioning, they are also based on real and present dangers for many. There are millions of people without access to clean water. There are girls afraid to go to school because they might be raped or killed. There are young men at risk of being shot by cops because of the color of their skin. There are well-educated, highly-paid professionals bankrupted by medical bills. There are middle-class workers made homeless by sudden job loss. There are parents paying off their own student debt while trying to save for children's college funds.

It would be dissociative to deny that these scarcity realities exist. We cannot bypass it by turning a blind eye. But the reason these unfortunate situations persist is *not* because we don't have enough. Let me repeat: it's not because we don't have enough. These realities persist because we have old-paradigm power structures that shortchange equality and justice. These realities persist because we have inefficient systems for global resource distribution. If we try to survive as independent individuals, separate families, or isolated nations, we can (and many do) starve. But when we share, there is always enough.

Show me the money and...

We commonly conflate abundance and money, but they are not the same thing. Abundance is an experiential quality associated with the free flow of energy. It is a flavor that we taste in our experience of life, and it may be more or less present in any given moment. When we tap into the frequency of abundance, we perceive that there is more than enough. More than enough money. More than enough everything. Abundance flows *through* us, not *to* us. It is a feeling of overflow, which has two faces: gratitude and generosity. We naturally expand our capacity for abundance when we start to see abundance as multi-dimensional. Abundance includes receiving support in the form of money and material resources, but it is not only that. It also encompasses all kinds of support.

Abundance of technical support

At times, our purpose work requires us to call upon gifts beyond our own. This is common, even when we are freely accessing the full range of our personal potential. In these times, we need to invite and receive support from the gifts of others.

When I was launching a crowdfunding campaign to support the production and publishing expenses for this book, I needed help with recording and producing a video. Gary Roberts is a freelance videographer who was serendipitously connected to me through my personal network. He supported me by making my campaign video. Similarly, I had originally planned to hire a graphic designer to render diagrams for this book. By chance, I met graphic facilitator Alina Gutierrez via Instagram, and learned that she could use her artistic talent to make hand-drawn illustrations. Both of these people brought important skills to support the creation of this book.

Abundance of emotional support

This may go without saying, but it is still worth saying — we need friends to lean on along the way. For this kind of support, the specific skill sets that they bring are less important. Their ability to be present and actively listen to us is more important. These are the people who can provide us with a safe place to vent, be our partner in commiseration as well as celebration, or act as an advisor to provide another perspective.

Throughout the book writing process, I was in almost daily contact with my friend Katie Mae. She contributed to the creation of the book both as an editor and contributor. But perhaps more importantly, she supported the internal process that I went through in becoming an author. Day in and day out, whether I was up or down, ecstatic or dejected, she witnessed, reflected, and supported me every step of the way.

Abundance of supporting connections

In the hyper-connected world that we live in, connections are currency. There's a lot of truth to the adage "It's not what you know, it's who you know." Another non-monetary form of support that we can receive is a connection to another human being; a link to another node in the web. The right connection, made in the right context and focused on the right content, is powerful for opening doors to opportunities.

In researching the four-part Venn diagram that was the precursor to my purpose flow model, I spent a lot of time trying to follow the internet trail back to the originator of that model, with no luck. What I didn't realize was that I was already connected with her on social media. Anais Bock and I were introduced virtually by a mutual friend who said, "you are both working with people on purpose — you two should meet." Later when I put out a general call for people to interview for my book, I found out that the person I was looking for all over the world wide web had already been in my personal network for more than a year.

Abundance of supporting insights

I attended a writers' retreat nearly a year before I began writing this book. I didn't have a book project in mind then, only a largely neglected blog, a few *Huffington Post* articles, and the intention to hone my writing craft. At that retreat, I was introduced to the idea of self-publishing by Brian Gruber, who would later become my writing coach. I had always thought that you had to have a publisher to write a book — in my mind, it was something that was only possible for established, experienced writers or public figures with massive social media followings. During a one-hour session that was part of that retreat, I published a 20-page e-book, *The Working On Purpose Workbook*. With Brian's guidance, I walked through the process step by step, and I saw my workbook immediately available for download on Amazon. This experience completely turned my perspective on publishing, upside-down. Suddenly, something that seemed impossible, was possible.

In the summer of 2018, I received a random Instagram message from a former business school classmate — someone I hadn't spoken to in a decade — asking, "Have you ever thought about writing a book?" She was starting a publishing company and she was looking for authors. The possibility of working together eventually withered after having an enthusiastic initial call. Yet a valuable seed was planted with that call. The thought was introduced that I might write a book, and someone might want to read it. This feedback from the world was filed away in a storage closet in my consciousness, where it would later start to grow and grab my full attention.

These moments of insight and inspiration were pivotal. I would certainly not be doing what I am doing right now without them. From the perspective of purpose, the abundance I received in the form of these ideas was more valuable to me than someone writing me a blank check. These ideas opened up avenues of possibility that were previously unimaginable to me.

Abundance includes much more than just money. When we access Abundance Flow, it is not restricted to a specific point in time or a specific place in space. It is non-local and non-temporal. Abundance energy is what supplies and sustains our personal resources. The feeling of being universally supported helps to fill our energy reserves and strengthen our resolve.

Four circles become one cycle

We have now expanded or adapted the definitions of the four static categories of the purpose Venn diagram to turn them into dynamic elements. We have also changed how these four elements interact. We no longer have four finite sets of things that overlap in some mysterious middle region. We are now looking at four dimensions of purpose that are connected in a single, circular, continuous flow.

We bring our Genius In Fluid Truth (GIFT) to bear in our creative response to life when we are tuned into the Personally Activating INformation (PAIN) that calls us to service. The response that organically emerges from loving presence is what helps us tap into Creative Flow as energy moves from the individual to the collective. To balance the cycle, this movement must come full circle. The world feeds back to us and fuels us when we are purpose-aligned. We receive resources and guidance from the collective, which inspire us to keep expanding the expression of our GIFT in the world. When we feel that sense of universal support, we experience Abundance Flow. What we receive from the world fills up our wellspring of love and inspires our creativity. This loop — between us as individuals and our collective reality — is infinitely regenerative.

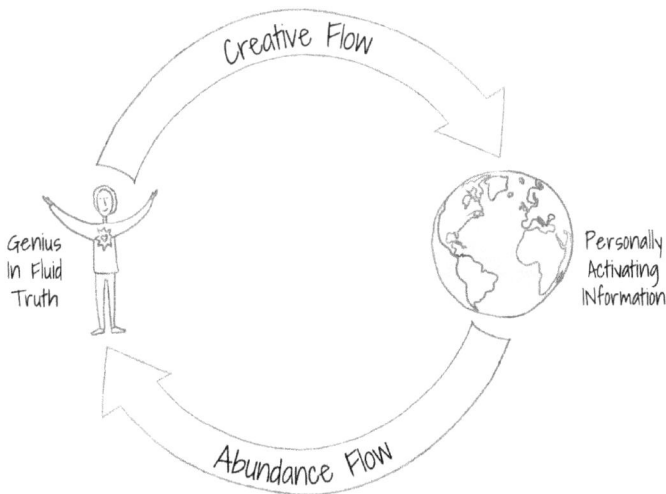

While these processes are illustrated as a cycle, they are not isolated phenomena taking place in stately sequence. They are interconnected dynamics that are happening simultaneously. We are looking into our inner sources of power at the same time that we are listening to our sensitivity to outer signals. We are responding to reality at the same time that we are inviting redirection. We are giving to the world at the same time that we are receiving support from it. It is all happening, all at once. We can choose to expand in any and all four of these dimensions to open ourselves to a more purpose-infused existence on Earth.

CHAPTER 4

The Four Core Purpose Qualities

A human being experiences himself, his thoughts and feelings, as something separate from the rest. This delusion is a kind of prison for us. Our task must be to free ourselves from this prison by widening our circle of compassion to embrace the whole of nature.
— **Albert Einstein**

Upon expanding the four dimensions of purpose, we start to step into a new paradigm of purpose work. We can see how purpose comes alive when four static categories are turned into four dynamic elements. A set theory problem becomes a regenerative flow cycle. We see how purpose moves through us, and how purpose moves us. But what comes next? What does it mean to follow a purpose path? How do we invite more purpose flow into our lives?

Regenerative purpose is not a finding; it is a feeling. We create unnecessary stress as we struggle to acquire and name a single purpose, in order to add it to our collection of accomplishments. By seeing that our existence is an expression of purpose, we can relax into connecting with it. We are not missing purpose. It is always already here, in the relational field between us and the rest of the world. Unfortunately, we are often blind to it, distracted from it, numb to it, or insensitive to it. But this is a symptom of the culture we live in. Old-paradigm structures and systems tend to disconnect us from nature, perpetuate obedience, and drive consumption. They distance us from an embodied sense of purpose. When purpose is externalized and objectified, it gets enrolled in supporting the old-paradigm program; it gets used as another trigger for lack and scarcity.

When we start to view purpose as an experience of personal evolution instead of as an object for personal acquisition, our energy and attention naturally shifts. Rather than looking for purpose outside, we start to look within.

Zen master Thich Nhat Han reflects on the importance of self-reflection and self-responsibility: "In Buddhism we speak of collective action. Sometimes something wrong is going on in the world and we think it is the other people who are doing it and we are not doing it. But you are part of the wrongdoing by the way you live your life."

The journey of regenerative purpose is fundamentally an inner work process. Our work on ourselves is naturally reflected in our work in the world. When we say yes to regenerative purpose, we begin to notice and nurture certain qualities in ourselves. The four core purpose qualities are: Authenticity, Attunement, Responsiveness, and Receptivity.

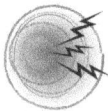

Authenticity   Attunement   Responsiveness   Receptivity

Qualities of being

Authenticity and Attunement are qualities of being that arise in stillness. They bring us to deeper presence, which awakens our energy, preparing and priming us for aligned action. There is a natural, magnetic attraction between the unique offerings that we have to give and the collective benefit that others can receive from them. Our gifts and the world's needs can be matched with greater ease when we embody a state of aliveness and awakeness. This state is enhanced by developing our qualities of being.

Authenticity is fully embracing the total truth of our selfhood. It is recognizing, owning, wielding, and nurturing the powers we hold, within the human container that we find ourselves in. It is a quality of being. It is a quality of "is-ness". No action is required to realize it.

Attunement is paying selective attention to the signals that affect us in certain ways. It infuses the way we attend to the conditions, situations, experiences, and information that are in our personal field of awareness right now. Attunement is not a movement; it is a state of awareness in stillness.

The qualities of Authenticity and Attunement tap into a truth that is both present and personal. These qualities of being help us stay connected with the truth of the present moment, as it is happening in our personal space.

Qualities of doing

Responsiveness and Receptivity are qualities of doing. They align the posture we assume when we act. When we embody these doing qualities, we engage and interact with the world by taking aligned actions, which often contribute to creating the experience of a flow state.

Responsiveness can also be referred to as Response-ability — meaning, the ability to respond. This quality allows us to touch what is alive in us, and give that treasure to the world. When we are strong in this quality, we take actions that exhibit a loving response rather than a fear-based reaction. We are able to move from presence.

Receptivity allows us to take in what is alive in the world. It lets us be touched by — and be moved by — what is going on around us. We are switched on and plugged in to collective intelligence when we are strong in receiving. The quality of Receptivity keeps us connected — recognizing ourselves as an individual node in the vast network of nature.

The qualities of Responsiveness and Receptivity support us to be purposefully aligned as we make our way through the world. As we make decisions, choose projects, or relate with others, Responsiveness and Receptivity help align our actions with forces of nature that exist within us and beyond us.

Authenticity expands our Genius In Fluid Truth (GIFT)

To be yourself in a world that is constantly trying to make you something else is the greatest accomplishment.
— **Ralph Waldo Emerson**

When we stand in Authenticity, our gifts start to be expressed as Genius In Fluid Truth (GIFT). Our GIFT includes the totality of basic raw materials we are given to build our lives with. For the blessings we are given to express their full potential, we must take stewardship of them. Stewardship means accepting the job of overseeing the maintenance, development, protection, and proper use of those gifts. This is where Authenticity comes in. When we are authentic, we are able to access more of our in-sourced potential.

Psychologists describe authentic people as demonstrating certain traits. They have realistic perceptions of reality. They accept themselves and other people. They are self-reflective. They express their emotions freely and clearly. They understand their motivations and are open to learning from mistakes. Authentic people are true to themselves. They are skilled at embodying and expressing their personal truth.

Authenticity aligns us with higher purpose. It acts a lot like a magnet. It attracts all the divine, delicious, beautiful things that are meant for us. And it is repellent to all the things that are not serving our purpose path. Authenticity is powerful. Why would we ever substitute our soul truth for the knock-off, bargain-basement version that is offered by our ego?

Our ego has good reasons for resisting being authentic. It might expose weakness. It might create conflict. It might be seen as morally defective. It might invite judgement. It might not earn us the approval we crave. We have endless reasons for not being authentic, which all come down to desires and fears that we have when relating with others.

Ultimately, the resistance we have to revealing our authentic self can be distilled down to one core fear: rejection. On a primal level, we need the acceptance and approval of our tribe to survive. Rejection avoidance is deeply-programmed, adaptive behavior. The paradox is that we must be willing to risk rejection — and even welcome it — in order to lead a purpose-full life.

Rejection is a side effect of being "out there" — it comes with exposing your heart and making yourself available to life.

Rejection is an elegant and efficient sorting mechanism, which helps us align and connect in the most beneficial way. Prolonged ambiguity leads to wasted time and leaked energy, whereas rejection enables us to spend time and energy more intelligently. Whatever you are holding onto by withholding your truth is only holding you back.

When we embrace the blessings of rejection, we reclaim energy that would otherwise be wasted on earning acceptance. When we stop trying to sell ourselves or convince people to love us, we have more to give to those who are ready to receive our gifts. When we ask for what we want without grasping for it, we allow the world to align with our true desires.

Rejection is the welcome mat where we wipe our feet as we walk through the door of opportunity. When we are authentic, only the truth can survive in our space. Those who do not share the same values or want the same things will fall away. Those who do, will come closer.

When we go into performance mode, we block energy by repressing our true expression. Performing is exhausting, whereas authentic expression is enlivening. These charades rob our lives of vital creative force. Having the courage to see and own our truth connects us with purpose flow. Cultivating Authenticity helps us activate our Genius In Fluid Truth.

Genius In Fluid Truth (GIFT) is blocked by identity fixation

Authenticity confronts a fixed sense of identity. To be more authentic, we need to see and release the identity anchors that drag us down. Identity draws a boundary line between who we think we are and who we think we are not. Identity helps us locate ourselves in the world, but it can also limit us.

We each carry around a bunch of ideas about who we think we are. These are beliefs in our self-image that we have inherited or developed over the course of our lives. We might see ourselves as a helpful friend, a responsible spendthrift, or a loyal employee. We might take on the persona of an irreverent rebel, a sexy temptress, or a wise teacher. No matter what our self-concepts are, they turn into traps when they get too fixed. We get used to presenting a certain version of ourselves to the world, and our place in that world feels secure as long as we play that predictable role. When we are stuck in a certain self-image, we limit our full expression in the living moment.

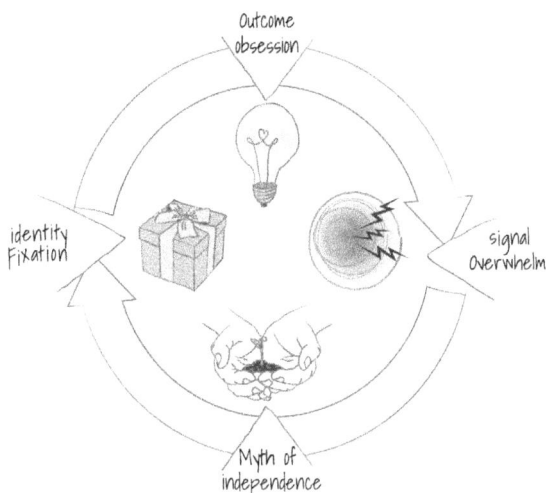

Identity is a shortcut for people to know how to relate to us. It helps our close friends, family members, colleagues, or casual acquaintances know what they can expect from us. In this way, our self-concepts are reinforced by relationships. We each have ways to find a safe station in the world. We hone these strategies over time and we keep using them because we know they work for us. The solidity of identity helps us maintain a stable society, but it's not very conducive to manifesting change.

The comfort we get from knowing who we are is also a confinement. Having too much certainty around our identity keeps us from opening to who we could become. If we want to grow, it's healthy to question our identity from time to time.

Both authenticity and identity can be described as "who we are." Identity, though, tends to be more fixed, less fluid. Identity is who we think we are, contained in a mental construct. It is an idea we hold onto to help us find our place. It is a role or a responsibility that we claim. It is the self-image that we project into the world. It helps us locate ourselves in the complex web of human connection. It gives us a rehearsed role to play. It gives us a reliable way to relate. It gives us a shortcut so we don't have to draw on a blank slate every day.

Identity offers a sense of security, but we have to release our attachment to this in order to welcome the arrival of authenticity. When our ideas about who we are remain too fixed, it limits us instead of liberating us. Tension comes if we feel beholden to maintaining a consistent image when the truth is changing — we will feel strained if we try to keep a straight face on the surface, while the substrate underneath is shaking and shifting. Authenticity is found in a fluid quality of engagement rather than in a solid state. It is how we show up in presence.

Dropping a fixed identity in favor of our fluid authentic nature can feel risky if it takes us outside the bounds of what is "normal" for us. Authenticity could mean pushing at the edges of what's socially approved, or it could mean trying on new approaches that don't play to known strengths. No matter how it shows up, when the truth of *who we are now* comes into conflict with *who we were before*, it is uncomfortable. This is why being authentic requires courage. We need courage when the fluid truth of who we are in the present moment flies in the face of others' impressions and expectations of us. There are risks associated with living our truth. Authenticity asks us to let go of safe behaviors that we fall back on from fear of rejection. The benefit of regularly re-examining everything that keeps our identity glued together, is that we can free ourselves to expand into more possible expressions.

Purpose flow feels good. When we experience it, it is natural to want to stay there, but we can only stay in the flow of purpose if we don't get attached to the form of our purpose. Fixed identity separates us from the truth of the present moment. Even if it is a purpose-driven identity, it still prevents us from being fully available to the never-ending stream of life's twists and turns. If we forget that, we get stuck standing in one place as purpose continues flowing around us. This is what happens when we get overly identified with our purpose.

The purpose of purpose is not to come up with a catchphrase that we can print on our ID card. The purpose of purpose is to access a state of activation and alignment that allows us to best serve. The purpose of purpose is to bring us into full, ecstatic, embodied engagement with life. If we manage to capture purpose and put it in a box, then purpose puts us in a box where we will stagnate if we stay.

When we get stuck in identity, we become an uninspired performer. We may create beautiful new things, address important problems in the world, and be paid well for our work, but if we lack Authenticity then we will ultimately feel empty. Even in playing a role well and giving a top performance, there is sadness in knowing it is not the true *you* coming through.

Attunement opens access to Personally Activating INformation (PAIN)

The real meditation is how you live your life from moment to moment. It's all relational. So, when you tune in to the body or the breath or sounds or smells or taste or touch or awareness of awareness, when you tune in in this way, it's a kind of relationship.
— **Jon Kabat-Zinn**

The pain we feel when we are in full contact with the world carries messages for us. It connects us to our calling in a relevant, actionable way. The purpose of pain is to act as a highlighter for us, it points us to a certain locus of focus. Pain collects and directs our attention — not so that we can suffer as the victim of circumstances, but rather so that we can become engaged and activated as the creative agents of change.

If the signals we allow into our system do not contain instructions for us; if the information we receive does not guide us towards acts of love; then those signals are simply useless noise. Allowing this noise to enter only drains our energy. When true signals reach us, we are led to take aligned action. To make pain something useful, to experience it as Personally Activating INformation, we must cultivate the quality of Attunement.

The dictionary definition of Attunement is twofold: one definition is to bring something into harmony or tune, the way you would tune an instrument; the other definition is to make someone or something aware and responsive. The quality that we are discussing here includes both definitions. For the purposes of purpose work, Attunement is listening deeply to the wisdom within us as it is evoked in our present-moment interactions with the world around us.

Attunement gives us the ability to filter information and focus our actions. Pain awareness is a critical part of purpose-alignment. Being attuned means that we have adjusted the dial on our personal radio receiver with an intention to listen for transmissions at a specific frequency. This kind of deep listening requires a higher level of attention than simply hearing; it is more present and more deliberate.

In the other three dimensions of the flow cycle, the core purpose quality is helping us expand: Authenticity enables us to better recognize and grow our unique gifts; Responsiveness increases our capacity to create and give; Receptivity increases our capacity to receive and flourish. But Attunement is different. The quality of Attunement is helping us narrow the scope rather than widen it. It helps us take in the vastness of the world and bring it into focus through a limited viewfinder.

What does it look like when we are attuned to receive relevant information that leads to action? Let's explore anger as an example of an activated state. Anger is a body signal that provides clarity around our boundaries. It tells us what we like and what we don't like; what we accept and what we reject; what is okay and what is not okay. Anger is powerful if we can access it and use it intentionally. Psychologists refer to anger as a "motivator for positive approach." In other words, anger is an activation energy that enables us to move towards creating what we desire, rather than moving away from what we fear.

The anger that we see on display in the public arena is largely toxic anger. It is brash, loud, dangerous, and destructive, the way that it is shown in Hollywood movies or depicted in sensational news media. Anger is represented in the form of virtual vitriol, verbal violence, or acts of physical aggression. This unhealthy anger is a weapon of indiscriminate destruction.

Healthy anger looks quite different from the mass media image of anger. Anger can be steady, centered, slow-burning, and constructive. To channel anger as a force of change, we need to intentionally engage without being emotionally reactive. As we listen to the guidance that anger provides, we learn where we need to direct our energy.

Consider these important differences between unhealthy and healthy anger:

Unhealthy anger...	Healthy anger...
• seeks to destroy what it stands against	• seeks to build up what it stands for
• clings to a disempowered, victim identity	• claims an empowered, creator identity
• casts blame on others for the past	• takes personal ownership for the future
• stubbornly defends its moral righteousness	• staunchly promotes its moral agenda
• is vague and unfocused in intention	• is clearly directed at a specific aim
• strives to exert control over other people	• requires sourcing power from within
• moves from a core of contempt	• moves from a core of compassion
• is energy that is dispersed when released	• is energy that is directed when expressed

The world could benefit from more constructive anger. When we connect with our inner wisdom and inhabit our true power, we stand in, instead of lash out. When we are grounded in our true self, there is no need to attack. Let's step into leadership that is fueled by the deliberate, directed power of healthy activation. The unmitigated rage of unhealthy anger basically amounts to disappointed and disempowered children screaming at each other. This is energy wasted. We need to grow up and channel healthy anger to power-up positive change.

Personally Activating INformation (PAIN) is blocked by signal overwhelm

In the data deluge of modern times, the information that we need to receive is often cancelled out or confused by signal overwhelm. Overwhelm hijacks the body-being to keep us enslaved in subservience to an outdated system. When we are attuned, we can use our life energy to serve humanity and higher purpose. But when we are overwhelmed, this signal interference prevents access to Personally Activating INformation.

To engage in purpose work in the world, we need to be in contact with the world. Our nervous systems can sometimes get flooded though, which leads to numbness or withdrawal. The world is cluttered with messages. We need to take protective measures against overload. With too much stimulation, we can easily miss the messages that are meant for us. Listening is how we learn where we can best serve. This means tuning our human instruments to be selectively sensitive; we want to receive and process *only* the signals that carry relevant data for us.

Consider how signal overwhelm has numbed us and taken us away from true engagement with life. We are constantly going through the motions of endless distraction, without effecting much real movement. For example, our response to tragedy has become pretty predictable and formulaic. A terrible thing happens. We feel shocked or sad. An outpouring of support or a storm of outrage circulates. It lasts for a New York minute. It moves us until we are drawn back into the mundane routine of our daily lives, or until our attention is diverted to the next new tragedy. Rinse, repeat. There's no real activation happening.

Attunement is supported by minimizing the interference of too many incoming signals. If you read the news today, you will see the daily variety show of scandals, assaults, shootings, hurricanes, fires, floods, and other disasters, natural and man-made. As journalist H.L. Mencken said a century ago, "A newspaper is a device for making the ignorant more ignorant and the crazy crazier." Even though we read fewer newspapers these days, we are immersed in digital media. Our blinking, buzzing, pinging, hand-held supercomputers are our constant companions. The ubiquity of information makes the hijacking of our attention even more pressing today. Once upon a time, fear was used to sell newspapers. These days, fear sells Facebook ads. Fear keeps us clicking and scrolling and consuming.

We can tune our body antennae to become more sensitive as a receiver of information. Information enters our space at an incredible volume and pace in our hyperconnected, always "on" modern world. From waking to sleeping, we are subjected to a non-stop flood of messages, notifications, ads, and invitations. It requires considerable discipline to manage and master our attention in this distraction-rich environment.

Aside from the sheer volume of signals, there is a negative bias to the signals we receive. Really, what keeps us clicking and scrolling is not the feel-good feature, it's the fatality count. Author Jeff Brown writes: "We are constantly assaulted with reminders of the horrors of humanity, while receiving little information about the kindness that is everywhere. Every day, our triggers are deliberately ignited by an institution that profits from sensationalism." The companies that want to sell us things are vying for our increasingly fragmented and limited attention. Psychological research tells us that stories provoking negative emotions grab our attention more than stories that inspire positive emotions. Advertisers use this to hook us.

We find another type of information infection in the health, beauty, and personal growth arena. These are all billion-dollar industries that flourish on a foundation of lack. They push sales by reinforcing an insatiable hunger for self-improvement, stemming from unworthiness or incompleteness. We feel compelled to try a new diet, buy a special skin cream, or enroll in a purpose discovery program because we fear we have some flaw that needs to be fixed; we feel we are missing something that needs to be found. Social media exacerbates this lack-trap by enlisting lack's faithful companion: comparison.

When we are triggered by the threat and lack sensations served up by the modern media machine, it is hard to pick up the important signals. If we are flooded with the daily barrage of messages that "the world is a scary place" and "you are not enough," then there is little space remaining for the meaningful messages that activate purpose. We need to develop Attunement to cut through the data clutter and tune into what matters.

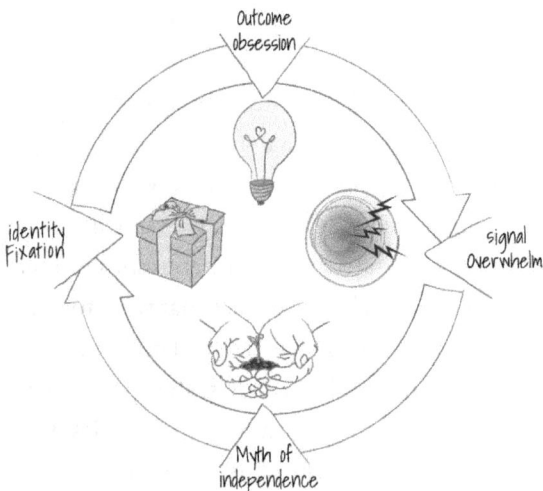

We need information so we can rally in the global town square. At the same time, we need to protect our sensitivity from being strung out by exposure to toxic media. Selective listening is critical for sensible action. Let's reflect on how reading the news serves us in taking actions that are positive and productive. How does it affect you to read article after article about the latest school shooting or scroll through endless pages of commentary about wildfires? Does it make you feel more inspired or more tired? Are you getting more engaged or just more enraged? Is the information activating or is it paralyzing?

In a state of overwhelm, we have Attunement blackout. We get mixed signals; we drift into confusion; we gravitate towards distractions for comfort. We may bring forth our authentic gifts, creatively forge new paths, and be well rewarded for our work, but if we are not tuned in to receive the most relevant and actionable messages for us, we become a blind activist. Championing change this way is often fraught with frustration. We pour a lot of energy into our purpose work, but we don't see the kind of impact we want because our energy is scattered in too many different directions.

Responsiveness expands our Creative Flow

We all say a lot of things about who we are and how we think. But in the end, it's your actions, how you respond to circumstance that reveals your character.
— **Cate Blanchett**

Creative Flow opens up to us when we develop our capacity for responding. Responsiveness is the quality we call upon to help us step out of patterned, programmed reactions. This is the quality that emerges when we fully inhabit the living moment. It is what happens when we exercise our individual will and express our creative imagination. We move from a feeling of fullness instead of fulfilling a role.

When we are creative, we are responding instead of reacting. Responding requires us to be rooted in presence, rather than acting out automatic behaviors. We are active without pushing for a particular outcome. When we respond creatively, we are able to come up with novel approaches to familiar situations. Responsiveness enables us to take aligned action. Aligned action is what we do when we are not merely repeating the reflexive, habitual actions that come from conditioning.

Our human supercomputer is simultaneously running many programs. A lot of these programs are really useful. We have a program that keeps our heart beating. We have a program that keeps our lungs breathing. We have programs that enable us to brush our teeth in the morning, drive ourselves to the supermarket, and feed our children. There are many things that we need to do in the course of daily life, which can be done on autopilot. Because we have these programs running, they don't consume a lot of mental energy. They get done more or less in the background, without a lot of processing power being used.

When it comes to purpose, we want to make choices from presence, not from programming. When we are present in our doing, what naturally pours forth is our expression of love.

Western education is generally designed to prepare humans for roles in an industrial economy, focused on manufacturing and selling physical products. That is true even if we have lived half of our lives in a largely post-industrial economy. In fact, the majority of humans alive today have been educated for work that is no longer relevant in our current reality. We continue to be educated for roles in an industrial economy, even as the world has shifted to become more and more of a service economy, an information economy, or even an energy economy.

Cultivating Responsiveness helps us access Creative Flow. Tapping into the flow of creation can seem renegade in the context of our conditioning. Maybe it's because the Western ideals of productivity and performance are so ingrained in us. We have strayed far from our original creative nature. We have widely-held misconceptions around what it means to be creative.

We often think of creativity as the exclusive purview of a specific sub-population. In the tech world, we have even turned the word "creative" into a noun. We refer to certain people or work groups as "creatives," perpetuating the idea that some people are creative and others are not. For example, artists, dancers, and singers are traditionally seen as creative. Yet all able-bodied humans can access these forms of expression. Saying "I am not creative" is a defense against internalized or anticipated judgement. What we are really saying is, "I am afraid that my creative expression is not 'good enough' according to an imaginary standard or authority." We give the power of our expression away. We give it away to an outsourced other who will decide its merit based on outcome. This constricts Creative Flow. It disconnects us from our creative nature. Our loving act of creation gets twisted into something else: performance made for consumption. True creativity is not about artistic prowess as much as it is about our ability to respond.

When we stop judging our creative output, we see that everyone has an artist, a dancer, and a singer in them. Besides, we can be creative in areas beyond visual art, movement, and music. We can be creative in business, in technology, or in medicine — truly in any human endeavor. Creativity is an enlivened quality that inhabits our actions; it emerges from us naturally when we respond from loving presence instead of reacting from fear-based programming.

When we cultivate Responsiveness, we are re-training ourselves to engage presence and disengage programming. We connect to Creative Flow when we are full of soul and empty of any goal. We are child-like. We plan less. We play more. We release our hold on executing a strategy and we let ourselves do things for no apparent reason. We bask in the sheer joy of exploring our place in the world and experimenting with our impact on the world. We embrace an attitude of "I wonder what will happen if we... let's try it and see!"

To invite Creative Flow, we need to rebel against the programs that have been installed in us. We have been taught to think linearly and logically. We have been trained to produce the same results repeatedly and efficiently. In a world where machines and computers can do most tasks better and faster than humans, it doesn't make sense for this to be our focus anymore. It is time for us to invest in our own re-education.

Creative Flow is blocked by generalized outcome obsession

What blocks Creative Flow is extreme goal-orientation. We fix our sights on a destination and then we strategize, we plan, and we toil to get there. If something is not working, we judge ourselves harshly for not getting there. We struggle because we work against nature. We are infected with the misguided belief that we can manipulate, control, and dominate nature. We think we can bend her to our personal will in the wrestling match of (hu)man vs. nature. In fact, I would say the dominant culture has gone beyond the outer reaches of goal-orientation and crossed over into the territory of *generalized outcome obsession.*

Our current paradigm is founded on linear and logical thinking. We are trained to perform based on the principles of individual achievement, single focus, and fierce competition for limited resources. We are taught that effort leads to performance and that performance leads to reward. We are applauded for reaching a goal or achieving a desired result.

What is lost in this generalized outcome obsession is the art of creation. We have forgotten how to play, how to explore, how to experiment. Creativity is the birthright of every human. Yet allowing creative expression to emerge is at odds with the cultural programming we have to focus on the finish line. It is not easy to break free from our achievement addiction and let go of our desire to control the outcome. It requires practice. It requires presence.

As I began writing this section of the book today, I received an email from a writing coach whose marketing list I am subscribed to. His message emphasized the value of having absolute clarity on what you want to achieve with writing a book. In the newsletter, he offers some examples of "practical, real-world destinations" for authors or aspiring authors:

- Over the next year, I want to get my book into the hands of 5,000 people.
- I want to book two speaking gigs of at least $2,000 per month, every month.

- I want 3 new clients a month, each paying me $5,000 to join my program.
- I want to at least double the revenue from my business while working with fewer one-on-one clients and leveraging my time working with groups.

For anyone writing a book, these are valid goals to have. When we are going somewhere, it can be useful to have a map. It's only when we get too attached to the achievement at the end of the road that we lose sight of why we started down this path in the first place. We are so focused on the pot of gold at the end of the rainbow that we miss the rainbow. It's good to be clear in our intentions, but we need to remain flexible about the form in which those intentions manifest.

Once we know the exact shape, size, color, and flavor of our intention, it's time to let it go. The difficulty there is that once we have a clear picture of what we want to create, the ego usually tries to take over and make it happen. That pressure to achieve creates anxiety. Too much attachment to a specific plan dulls our creativity. Our desire for a certain result can ruin ease and restrict flow. Instead we want to stay focused on what is in front of us, here and now. When we catch ourselves looking too far out on the horizon or worrying too much about what will happen, we need to come back to the present moment. Taking one step at a time, we surrender our personal will to greater intelligence. We must trust that the best outcome is what will come.

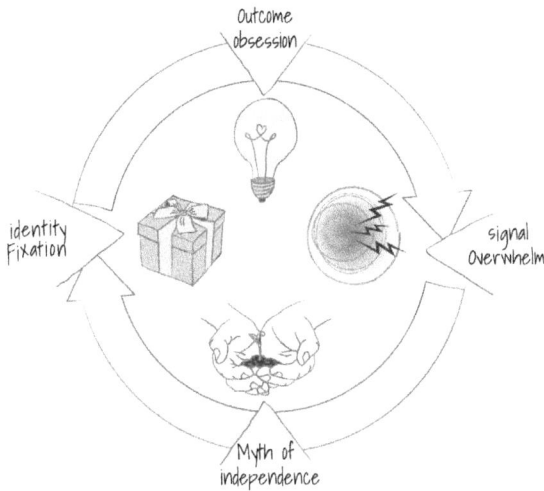

When we find it hard to trust, sometimes it helps to look back and remember how we got to where we are now. Things probably unfolded slowly and surely. The path never ends; it only evolves. New paths always reveal themselves on the way. There's no final place "there" for us to get to. Once we arrive at the imagined "there," even more possibilities present themselves to us. The accumulation of all those "now's" does lead us somewhere, but not necessarily to where we planned or predicted. Sometimes, it's somewhere even better! Obsessing about specific outcomes makes us miss out on unexpected opportunities. But when we channel our devotion in the present moment, step by step, the way reveals itself.

When we can find the delicate edge where we hold clear intentions yet remain open around the outcome, that is where the magic happens. This is the space where Responsiveness reigns. The kind of action that arises here is gentle and effortless. It is not pushy or labored. We show up joyfully to where we are invited. We make unexpected new connections. We embrace new perspectives. We take in new experiences with ease.

When we are too focused on the outcome, our creative capacity shrinks. We may express our soul truth, listen to what the world needs, and feel guided and supported in our work — but without accessing Creative Flow, we are less connected with our humanity. We become the mechanical miser. There is a robotic quality to the way that we do things. Our actions start to feel boring and meaningless because we are miserly in withholding the full spectrum of our potential.

Receptivity opens access to Abundance Flow

> *Until we can receive with an open heart,*
> *we're never really giving with an open heart.*
> *When we attach judgment to receiving help,*
> *we attach judgment to giving help.*
> **— Brené Brown**

When we access Abundance Flow, we receive, rather than reject, the resources that we recognize as being "we"-sources. We feel connected, not separate. We are sustained by interdependence instead of striving for independence. We surrender to service without feeling sacrificed for the sake of service. Cultivating Receptivity helps us access Abundance Flow.

Now, I know that we all want to know: how can I get my purpose work to *pay* me? If making money is your main concern, then you may be reading the wrong book. Before we continue our discussion of how developing Receptivity invites abundance, it may be useful to distinguish between two often confused terms: "manifesting abundance" and making money.

"Manifesting abundance" is a new age phrase that has become so overused, its original meaning has been twisted beyond recognition. We have a massive misunderstanding about what it means to manifest abundance. Abundance does not need anyone to make it happen. Abundance already is. To "manifest" means to make something apparent; it does not mean to make something happen. (To read my take on manifesting, see the bonus content: "The Real Secret to Manifesting.")

Abundance is what we experience when we are in harmony with nature. Our separation from abundance is separation from nature, reinforced by a system that profits from our fear and scarcity. You may receive money with more ease when you feel a sense of abundance. You may experience a sense of abundance when money comes to you. However, manifesting abundance — that is, abundance becoming more apparent — is not equivalent to making money.

Abundance is a frequency or vibration. It adds a certain richness to the flavors that are present as we taste the experience of life. It is an energetic current that is available for us to access at any time. It's not something that we can manage, manufacture, or measure. Money, on the other hand, is a material form. We can and do acquire it, quantify it, hoard it, or distribute it.

Abundance is...	Money is...
• Frequency	• form
• infinite, limitless	• finite, limited
• vibrational, energy	• physical, matter
• experienced as a quality	• measured in quantity
• always available to access	• sometimes present to steward

My definition of abundance is: the space that exists between (a) what-you-think-you-need and (b) what-you-think-you-have. These two concepts mark the boundary edges of the space of abundance. These ideas create the limits that cause contraction or constriction of Abundance Flow. The good news is that both boundaries are mind-created concepts. This means that we can experience more abundance simply by changing our mindset — by seeing that we have more than we used to think or by seeing that we need less than we used to think.

Money, on the other hand, is material, physical reality. It does not magically fall out of the sky from us vibrating, visualizing, waving a magic wand, or wishing on a star — even though those things *can* support us to be more aligned in our money-making activities. Money is a means for actualizing our creative expression. On its own, money does not hold positive or negative charge. It is an empty container for the energy that we put into it. Money can carry a frequency of abundance and generosity, or it can carry a frequency of scarcity and greed.

You can have lots of money without experiencing abundance. There are plenty of people in the world who have huge amounts of money and have no clue what abundance is.

The opposite is also true. You can experience abundance without having lots of money. That said, while we're here in human form, most of us still need to use money in our daily lives. Unless you're living completely off the grid — generating your own energy, growing your own food, and processing your own waste — then money is necessary. No, it is not a necessary *evil*. Money is not inherently evil.

Money is something that we have lots of stories and distortions around. It is a symbolic object that we have tied to power, respect, status, and safety — among other things. There is a lot of collective wounding when it comes to money — its creation, its control, its uses, and its distribution. We do need to address all this to come into right relationship with money.

What we do *not* need to do is Light-wash our money-making activities with a spiritual brush. Receiving money is not something to be ashamed of. Generating income is not something vulgar or impure. When wielded with love, money is powerful currency for positive change. It is merely a medium for translating our highest visions into physical reality. It turns love into matter. We don't need to call money by the name of abundance to make it more spiritually acceptable. Instead, let's reclaim money from the shadow of shame and make it sacred again. Let's take back the power of money and steward it with utmost integrity for the sake of higher purpose.

We can manifest abundance *and* make money. We can appreciate abundance, and also, generate income. We can reveal abundance, and also, earn cash. Abundance and money are not the same, and they are not mutually exclusive.

To develop our Receptivity, we have to unsubscribe from the story of separation and self-sufficiency. Receiving is what keeps us connected to the web of life that weaves us all together. We see how we are tied together by these invisible threads, and we see how our active participation in the web of life is necessary in order to continue the cycle of creation. Allowing ourselves to be guided and supported is what makes our purpose work both impactful and sustainable. Purpose work is our soul mission, but if we are to thrive, it cannot be our solo mission.

Brandon Peele shares how Receptivity brings more:

I have spent most of my life pitched forward at a 15-degree angle. You can even see it reflected in my posture. Every time I catch my reflection, I have to remind myself, "hey, shoulders back." I would say that receptivity is something I'm cultivating. It hasn't been easy, but it's starting to come online. I am allowing others to contribute to me and my work, and I am trusting more and more that everything is okay. I am relaxing in knowing that the next thing is going to come and it's going to be perfect. I don't have to go out and find it. I'm trying to inhabit more of this posture of reclined peace instead of being this warrior that is out to expand the kingdom, and it's just been beautiful. I'm starting to have more to show for it — things are starting to come in. It's interesting how you can do less and there's more.

Abundance Flow is blocked by the myth of independence

What gets in the way of Abundance Flow is the myth of independence. In our modern reality, where we can meet many needs by tapping an app on a smartphone screen, it's easy to forget how much we depend on nature's resources and how much we rely on other humans. To expand in the quality of Receptivity, we have to give up the belief that the pinnacle of success is independence.

In the Western world, we prioritize and even pride ourselves on owning our own everything. Our own house. Our own car. Our own television. Our own wedding dress. Our own lawn mower. Our own baby stroller. Our own scuba gear. We acquire and accumulate loads of physical stuff over time without even noticing. We are encouraged from a young age to function independently of other people. We are taught to find safety in not needing anything from anyone. We get so busy procuring things for me, myself, and mine that we don't even stop to think about how or why we are doing it. We never pause to question the assumption of independence.

The myth of independence leads to the overproduction and overconsumption of physical stuff that we don't actually need. It keeps us from experiencing the truth of abundance that exists in nature. We need to renegotiate our relationship with resource and repair our connection with community if we want to restore our access to Abundance Flow. We need to acknowledge and celebrate our interdependence.

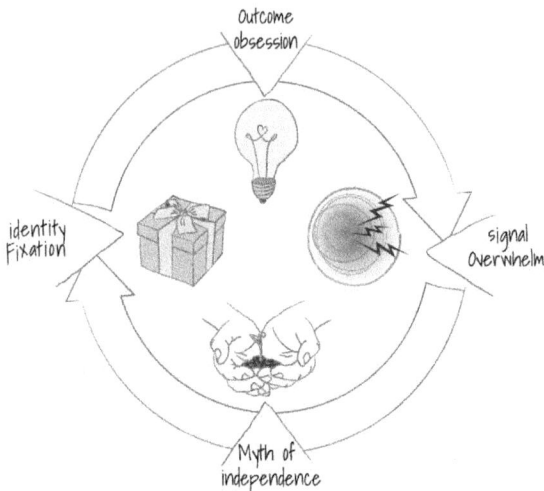

Independence breeds disconnection in many dimensions. These ills (truly, illnesses) are rooted in our dysfunctional relationship with resource. With globalization, we are more and more removed from the sources of production for all the things that we consume. This means that we are more disconnected from Mother Earth; we are more disconnected from other human beings; we are more disconnected from ourselves; and ultimately, we are more disconnected from life.

Charles Eisenstein shares a compelling vision for righting our relationship with resource: "When we must pay the true price for the depletion of nature's gifts, materials will become more precious to us and economic logic will reinforce, not contradict, our heart's desire to treat the world with reverence and, when we receive nature's gifts, to use them well."

It's a nice idea — that we might one day have economic systems that mirror and support our natural systems. But we are definitely not there yet, and for those of us who are leading the charge to make changes to the current system, it takes a lot of courage to leap into that gap.

Money fear is the number one reason why my coaching clients procrastinate on their purpose path. The fear that there won't be enough money (whatever enough means) creates a debilitating internal narrative. Of course, it helps to have a solid financial foundation. It is easier to takes risks and explore new things when we feel a certain amount of financial safety and financial freedom. However, money is not the cure-all. Even those who have a lot of material wealth can be paralyzed by the possibility of financial doom.

Money fear touches everyone, regardless of socioeconomic status. We believe that we never have enough, or that we always need more. Scarcity mindset doesn't discriminate according to our bank balance — because this fear is rooted in the state of our separation, not in the state of our savings account. When we are separated from Mother Nature and estranged from the global family of humanity, we are constantly seized by the fear of not having enough that is "mine."

When we are caught in the lack trap, by default we have adopted an individualistic approach to resource acquisition. The shift to a collectivist approach invites us to consider resource access instead. Seeing resources as "we"-sources, we start to prioritize community care as much as we pride ourselves on self-care. Family therapist and resilience researcher Michael Ungar makes a strong case for attending to community care rather than relentlessly focusing on self-improvement:

> *Resilience is not a DIY endeavor. Self-help fails because the stresses that put our lives in jeopardy in the first place*

remain in the world around us even after we've taken the "cures." The fact is that people who can find the resources they require for success in their environments are far more likely to succeed than individuals with positive thoughts and the latest power poses. What kind of resources? The kind that get you through the inevitable crises that life throws our way. A bank of sick days. Some savings or an extended family who can take you in. Neighbors or a congregation willing to bring over a casserole, shovel your driveway or help care for your children while you are doing whatever you need to do to get through the moment. Communities with police, social workers, home-care workers, fire departments, ambulances, and food banks. Employment insurance, pension plans or financial advisers to help you through a layoff.

Independence may generate wealth but interdependence is what invites abundance. We are part of a living mandala, each one weaving a thread into the fabric of humanity. The decisions of every individual impact the collective, and the decisions of the collective influence every individual. The truth is, we can be sovereign without being separate. Receptivity open us up to this truth. The future health of the planet depends on us coming to this realization.

When we are busy believing in the myth of independence, we keep ourselves from fully receiving what is available. We become the proud martyr. We might embrace our authentic self, creatively express ourselves, and be activated by our unique sensitivity in the world, but without expanding our ability to receive, our purpose work is not sustainable. If we fail to cultivate

Receptivity, we will limit Abundance Flow. If we let ourselves languish there, we are prone to building up resentment and eventually, experiencing burnout.

The eternal cycle of purpose flow

As we continue to develop the four core purpose qualities, we will start to experience purpose more profoundly and more persistently. Purpose *wants* to move through us. It is our nature. There is nothing special that we need to do to make purpose happen. Purpose always finds a path, with time. If it doesn't move through you, it will move through someone else. Purpose doesn't have an opinion about you. It doesn't mind whether you decide to play, or prefer to stay away. If you are not participating, it will find another way.

We are not missing purpose, but purpose can miss us. We invite purpose flow to move through us because we want to come fully, vibrantly alive. We want to create and contribute. We want to take our place in the family of humanity. We want to do more than survive until we die. We want to live magical, meaningful, and rich lives. We can intentionally remove blocks that prevent purpose from moving as we cultivate the four core purpose qualities. Our expansion in these dimensions helps us step into the flow of purpose.

Genius In Fluid Truth (GIFT) gives rise to the signals that radiate from us and Personally Activating INformation (PAIN) highlights the signals that touch us. The individual and collective elements are participants in a purpose conversation. They are always putting out transmissions. Like radio signals, sometimes the signals are strong and sometimes they are weak, or distorted by interference. We keep the channels of communication open and clear by cultivating Authenticity and Attunement. The full potential of our GIFT can only be expressed when we embody Authenticity. The ways and places we can best serve reveal themselves to us when we demonstrate Attunement.

Creative Flow and Abundance Flow are the movements of the purpose flow cycle, which represent an exchange of energy between the individual and the collective elements. When we can both respond and receive, we take aligned actions that express our unique self, while serving something universal. Having balance in responding and receiving helps sustain the cycle. Love flows freely in both directions. As we grow more skillful in Responsiveness, Creative Flow elevates the impact of what we share with the world. When we increase our capacity for Receptivity, the Abundance Flow that we receive from the world nourishes us to continue.

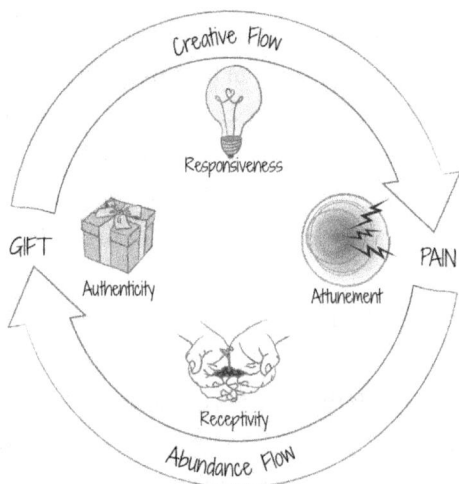

CHAPTER 5

The Layers of Unfolding and Integration

I began to see that the mandala is a way of seeing the world. I particularly liked the idea that the mandala doesn't need to be constructed or organized, that our world in all its apparent chaos is actually a spontaneous, ever-evolving mandala.
— **Lama Tsultrium Allione**

Each of the four core purpose qualities — Authenticity, Attunement, Responsiveness, and Receptivity — has layers that reveal the processes of unfolding and integrating that are inherent in them. These layers describe how the qualities unfold from our inner core into outer form, and how worldly reality integrates into our deeper being. Each of the four purpose qualities has three layers: an inner layer, outer layer, and an interface layer in between, where the inner and outer worlds meet.

Layers of Authenticity

There are three postures that support us in cultivating Authenticity, as it spirals outward, unfolding from our inner world to the outer world. The three layers of Authenticity are: self-acceptance, congruence, and truthfulness.

- *Self-acceptance* (inner layer) is recognizing and embracing the wholeness of who/how we are: "I give myself permission to be everything I am."
- *Congruence* (interface layer) is the consistency and continuity between our inner experience and outer expression: "I am who I am without compromise."
- *Truthfulness* (outer layer) is the expression of our authentic self when we come into contact with the world: "I share the totality of me."

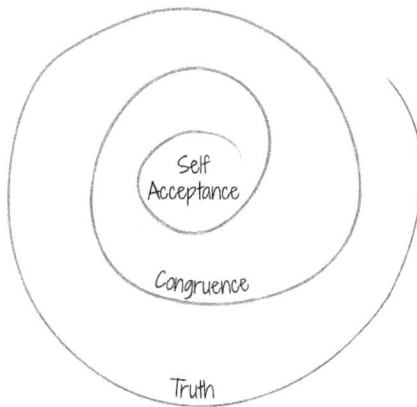

Self
Acceptance

Congruence

Truth

Self-acceptance (Authenticity: inner layer)

The inner layer of Authenticity is self-acceptance. The ability to take on board the entirety of ourselves is the inner core of this quality, from which Authenticity is sourced. Authentic people embrace more of their collection of talents, circumstances, and experiences. Most of us proudly display the bright, shiny things in our collection and struggle to cover up the dark, twisted things. We tend to see the shiny things as assets and the shadowy things as liabilities. Authenticity asks us to accept everything we get in our basket of gifts, and in this acceptance, we see how all our gifts can be alchemized into assets.

We are conditioned to hide certain things from others, and even from ourselves. The process of revealing and recovering more of our whole self is sometimes called shadow work. Carl Jung introduced the concept of the shadow in psychology, using it to refer to an aspect of our personality that is unseen. Shadows are often associated with darkness. Because of this, shadows are often seen as something bad. While it's possible that some real or perceived judgment of these parts of us as being bad is what led to them being hidden in the first place, shadows are not necessarily negative. As soon as a shadow aspect is brought into conscious awareness, it is no longer a shadow because it is no longer hidden.

Diving into our shadows, we open the possibility of collecting the forgotten, neglected, and rejected pieces of ourselves. Though, seeing our shadows in an instant of insight is not that useful for cultivating Authenticity. This process can only support us in becoming more wholly authentic when we integrate these previously unseen parts. Insight can happen in seconds. Integration usually takes a while longer, since it requires that we not only see our shadow aspects but also accept and own them. We must recognize our shadows and lovingly reclaim them as part of the wholeness of us, instead of disowning them as if they were the hole in us.

Women's leadership coach Nisha Moodley says, "We are in a time of profound healing. Those who will lead humanity's way forward are the ones most willing to show up all the way and stay the course to do the work. Hint: the work is wholeness."

In order to fully accept ourselves, we often have to overcome shame. Habits of shame are sticky. We have so much to overcome in breaking habits of hiding, disowning, or disconnecting from parts of ourselves. Shame is pervasive. Shame is also a profitable marketing strategy. White women buy bronzers and self-tanners to get that never-ending, beach vacation, "lady of leisure" look. Meanwhile, Asian women buy skin products full of chemical whitening agents to get that precious porcelain doll complexion.

It doesn't matter who you are: every minute, we are being sold ways to edit, enhance, and improve ourselves. We are bombarded with the message that who we are and how we are is not quite right or not quite enough. If you appreciate meta-level irony, you might see how it's possible to pick up this book with that orientation, in search of self-improvement.

Self-acceptance is the inner layer of Authenticity. It is at the heart of this quality. The ability to see and embrace everything that we are — good, bad, and ugly — is foundational to becoming more authentic.

Congruence (Authenticity: interface layer)

We demonstrate congruence when we are in integrity with ourselves. Congruence is the layer where the quality of Authenticity gets tested. Our authentic expression can only be manifested when we carry ourselves in a way that is internally and externally consistent. We must take actions according to our values. Our behaviors must align with our beliefs. Our decisions must support our deepest desires. Our choices must resonate with our inner voices. Externally, we must walk our inner talk.

When congruence is lacking, we experience inner conflict or cognitive dissonance. This is the aspect of Authenticity that is tested when we make contact with the outside world. Most of us experience some degree of dissonance every day. We edit ourselves to fit into the box that society draws around us. We swallow our truth to show up appropriately. We do what is expected to fulfill social contracts. This is why it can be helpful for people going through personal transformation to remove themselves from everything they know for some time. Usually, we have partner demands, family obligations, work standards, societal norms, and cultural constructs creating a cacophony of context around us. In an environment without familiar context, we can more easily hear our own voice. Congruence means developing the ability to hear and trust our internal voice, even when the external noise is deafening.

Congruence is the interface where the inner and outer layers of Authenticity meet. It is the friction point of this quality. As social creatures, sometimes it is appropriate and advantageous for us to conform to the demands of our external reality. In this way, the cultivation of congruence is a delicate dance. What naturally happens as we become more consistently connected with our inner truth, is that we start to align with the outer world only when our presence serves higher purpose.

Truthfulness (Authenticity: outer layer)

Truthfulness is how we touch the outside world by sharing our authentic self. This is the outer layer of Authenticity, where the authentic self becomes apparent to others. It is the layer where the quality of Authenticity is externally expressed.

We live in relationship with other humans. In fact, most of us are engaged in multiple relational fields, all at the same time. We are constantly involved in social and economic contracts of exchange. Truthfulness is how Authenticity shows up in these interpersonal dynamics.

Truthfulness can be a mischievous thing. We might think we are telling the truth when in fact, our ego is up to something else. We might believe we are authentic when we are actually acting out an unhealthy pattern. It is not always obvious when we are expressing deep, soul-spoken truth, and when we are performing a false, ego-driven truth. Learning the difference between the two helps us become more authentic and bring forth more of our deepest gifts.

We are not talking about absolute, universal truth here. We are talking about the subjective, personal truth that speaks from the seat of the soul. This is your truth, and my truth. This is the individual truth that belongs to I/you/me. It is not the collective truth of they/them/we. Soul truth is *personal* — it is wholly specific to each unique human being.

When we look at our personal truth, we are vulnerable to ego-based distortions. We need to recognize when our expression is coming from a deeper, soul-sourced well of truth or from a self-serving egoic drive. The soul truth liberates and enlivens us. The ego, on the other hand, manufactures a cheap imitation of that truth, which restricts and deadens us. This ego-based imitation of the truth will lead us away from Authenticity. There are a few ways we can distinguish the soul truth from the self-serving, ego-created variety:

- *Soul truth has no agenda.* If in speaking our truth, we are pursuing a specific outcome, we need to be wary. Our authentic expression pours forth like a waterfall cresting a cliff because it sees no other option than to express itself as life itself. It does not make itself seen and heard with an objective in mind. Soul truth shines through *in spite of* egoic concerns we have about maintaining a certain public image. It is the shining truth that radiates from within, regardless of egoic fears that others might disapprove or disagree.

- *Soul truth is self-centering.* Soul truth is not "self-centered" in the sense of being self-absorbed, inconsiderate, or narcissistic. However, it is self-centering because it requires us to be centered within ourselves. Soul truth is self-centering because it emerges from our own subjective experience. Soul truth makes "I" statements rather than "you" statements. It does not make assertions about outside events, or assumptions about others. Authentic expression is internally sourced. It is an outer expression of an inner discovery.

- *Soul truth is impermanent.* An expression of soul truth exists only in presence. It is true for one unique person, at one particular point in time. It is moment specific. Our authentic truth is a living, breathing, moving, and morphing thing. You cannot capture it or put a box around it because the moment it is expressed, there is the possibility that it will change.

We recover and recognize more of our authentic selves by strengthening a foundation of self-acceptance. We reconcile inner conflicts by attending to congruence. Then when we come into contact with the world, truthfulness enables us to engage with reality by expressing our authentic voice. Developing these layers of Authenticity supports us to reveal a greater store of our treasures to the world.

Layers of Attunement

There are three postures that support us in cultivating Attunement, as it spirals inward, integrating from our outer reality into our inner being. The three layers of Attunement are: engagement, discernment, and guidance.

- *Engagement* (outer layer) is showing up and sensing the world around us: "I am available to be touched by life."
- *Discernment* (interface layer) is filtering the inputs that we receive: "I choose where to focus my attention."
- *Guidance* (inner layer) is allowing the information we take in to give us direction: "I receive instructions from my conversation with reality."

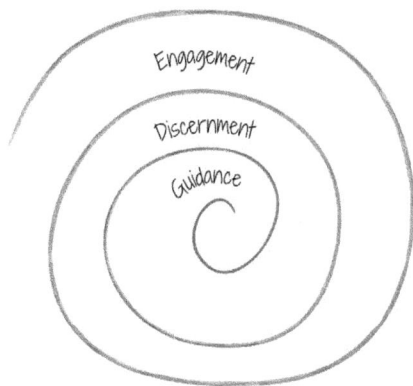

Engagement (Attunement: outer layer)

The outermost layer of Attunement is engagement. This is where this quality starts. To receive relevant signals from the world, we need to be engaged with life. Most of us know what it feels like to be disengaged from life. We show up at work for a paycheck. We show up at a party for social approval. We show up at dinner to meet a family obligation. We walk around numbed out, performing the motions of our lives. When we are in this mode, there's a lot of energy dispersed in pointless distraction, but not much movement in a particular direction.

When the world feels like *too much*, it is normal to want to retreat to our sanctuary or switch off our sensitivity. We all harbor defense mechanisms that have hardened around past trauma. We all carry some sense of learned helplessness, built up from all the times we put forth our best effort without seeing any impact. On some level, numbing and withdrawing is a smart strategy. It is an effective way to protect us against the "ouch" of painful experiences, the hurts that we risk suffering if we allow ourselves to feel life deeply.

Engaging with life is risky. We expose ourselves by engaging. Yet only when we are active participants in the adventure of life can we feel fully alive and aligned on our purpose path. We cannot listen to music through a radio that has been switched off. We also cannot receive the signals of our calling when our antennae are retracted in self-protection. Choosing to engage means making ourselves vulnerable. But if we want to experience purpose flow, we have to make ourselves available for life to reach us.

Discernment (Attunement: interface layer)

Discernment is the interface layer of Attunement, where the outer world and inner world meet. It is the friction point of this quality. This is where we filter the information that is coming in. How do we know what to pay attention to? How do we selectively focus? It is easy to get distracted or overwhelmed these days. But we must be discerning. Narrowing our focus increases our impact. We are all multi-potentiate beings, but we cannot do all the jobs that need to be done at once. We are a single cell in a complex, multicellular organism. When cells specialize in a specific function within a larger organism, they are more effective in contributing to the whole. It's true that we are all in this mess together, but to make ourselves useful to life, we need to learn to mind our own business better.

Discernment is different from the mind-directed focus that obsesses about achieving a future goal. Discernment is a heart-informed filtering process; it's about taking care with where we spend our energy in the present moment. Focus typically enlists us to push forward towards a specific destination, whereas discernment enlivens an area of devotion. Discernment moves us to pour our love into one form, as preferred over another, for a determined period of time. It channels our efforts into the cause or creation that makes us come alive here and now.

We need to have discernment because even though we can care about everything, we simply cannot carry everything that we care about. Singer-songwriter Fia Forsström makes a fierce case for the benefits of discernment.

> *I am a superhero but my job is not to fix the whole world. Our differences are strengths. The pull we feel to be and serve in different ways and places is designed with divine precision — and when acted upon, we unlock wisdom and access new energy needed for further evolution. Just because I am not climbing the fences and marching the streets, it does not mean that I do not care. Just because I am not traveling to poor countries and supporting communities in person, it does not mean that I do not care. Just because I am not writing about*

animal rights and I am not out there freeing caged creatures,
it does not mean I do not care. I stay in my lane. I do things
in a way that will allow my excellence to have the biggest
impact. I focus and direct my energy in the exact places I feel
are asking for my light. That is not turning a blind eye. That
is self-awareness. So let us ditch the separation, tearing people
down for not fighting our specific cause and instead take that
energy and turn it inwards, allowing it to fuel our fire and
start taking full responsibility for ourselves and what we are
weaving into the collective web of consciousness.

Discernment helps us block out noise and distractions. It helps us consciously collect our energy and put it into a container instead of letting it scatter to the winds. Whereas mind-directed focus is more intent on pursuing something that we want, heart-informed discernment is more involved in filtering out the things we don't want. Discernment helps us take our energy back from the vortex of distractions that swirl around us.

Guidance (Attunement: inner layer)

Guidance is the innermost layer of Attunement where the information we receive is translated into instructions. This is where the quality of Attunement is integrated into the core of our being. When we are available to be touched by life and able to discern what signals to pay attention to, it naturally creates an activation within us. That activation is guidance for us.

When we feel pain, we reflexively direct our attention to where that pain is located. We may label this attention as anger or some other strong emotion, but at the root, it is simply activation. Activation is the natural response to experiencing pain because we don't like pain and we want to make it go away. Pain acts like a highlighter; it points us to what we need to pay attention to. An immense amount of information passes through our system every day, but it fades unless it lights a fire in us. The sensations that we are most sensitive to are indeed giving us guidance by provoking us.

There is intelligence in our emotional response to what is going on around us. The emotions we label as negative are often the ones that contain the most potent information for us. As author Sara Sophia Eisenman writes, "There is not a single emotion or emotional state — not sadness, not grief, not lust, not rage, not shame, not jealousy, not even hatred — that is in and of itself 'negative' or 'toxic'. All emotions are messengers and agents of transformation, and it is how we choose to be with them, heed their messages, and let them work their magical change in us (or not), that makes the difference."

In other words, our sensitivity serves as a personal guidance system. We often tend to suppress negative emotions such as pain, grief or anger. But when we turn away from these emotions, we miss out on important messages and we waste the powerful activation energy that comes with them.

Guidance is the innermost layer of Attunement. This is the layer where information from the world is integrated into our inner being. Guidance comes from the activation we experience while in conversation with reality. When this fire is sparked deep within our hearts, we intuitively know where to invest our energy as a force for creation.

The ability to receive information, filter and sort it, and ultimately find guidance in it, is important and necessary. In cultivating the quality of Attunement, we become more sensitive to information that is meant for us. We are able to hear the messages that help guide our individual actions so we can show up where we are uniquely designed to serve.

Layers of Responsiveness

There are three postures that support us cultivating the quality of Responsiveness, as it spirals outward, unfolding from our inner world to the outer world. The three layers of this quality are: sovereignty, curiosity, and playfulness.

- *Sovereignty* (inner layer) is the foundational freedom we feel in our inner world: "I know I can choose."
- *Curiosity* (interface layer) is a sense of openness at the point where our inner and outer worlds meet: "I wonder how I will impact the world."
- *Playfulness* (outer layer) is an attitude of willingness to embrace possibility in the outer world: "I will try it out!"

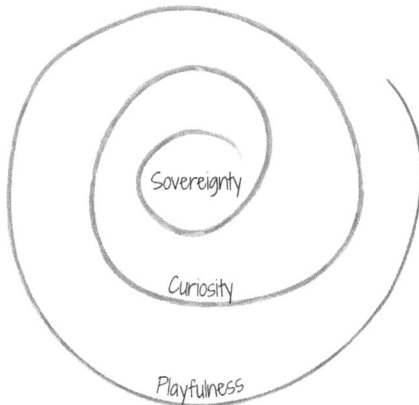

Sovereignty (Responsiveness: inner layer)

Sovereignty is the inner layer of Responsiveness. This is the inner core from which the quality of Responsiveness is sourced. At the core of our ability to respond, we must believe that we are a creator of our personal reality, not a victim of our personal history. We are inherently creative as human beings. We have the ability to form new neural pathways. We have the capacity to dream and imagine new paradigms for the way things might be — instead of succumbing to the way they have always been. Owning our sovereignty means quieting the part of the mind that says: "I have seen this movie before and I know how it ends." Instead, we take a seat in the director's chair. From there, we can look upon an old scene with fresh eyes and write a new narrative.

You may know the story of *The Little Engine That Could*, whose motto was "I think I can, I think I can." This fable teaches us about the power of the mind. Of course, it takes more than wishful thinking to make changes in our lives. Yet, we're often engaged in mental habits that keep us stuck somewhere we'd rather not be. We stay there because it's comfortable, without even noticing the thoughts that are holding us in place.

How often have you told yourself you can't? You can't upset your boss. You can't disappoint your family. You can't take time out for yourself. You can't be alone. You can't take a pay cut. You can't move to a new city. You can't possibly risk loving so much. A simple and subtle mind shift can create our reality anew. The next time the thought "I can't" arises in your mind, you can transform it into "I choose" instead.

- "I can't quit my job," becomes "I choose financial security for myself and my family."
- "I can't commit to this project," becomes "I choose to embrace flexibility and freedom."
- "I can't move to a new city," becomes "I choose the

comfort of familiar surroundings."

Owning the choices that you make is embracing sovereignty. This is empowering because you are in the director's chair calling the shots. True, inner-sourced power comes from putting yourself in that seat. You see that you are choosing in this moment, even if your current choices represent compromises. You recognize your agency. With this recognition comes the richness of possibility as you realize the impermanence of your choice. Whatever your current situation is, it is not a fixed statement of fact. You need not accept it as reality forever. Speaking about choices in the present tense opens the potential to make different choices in the future.

Curiosity (Responsiveness: interface layer)

Adopting a posture of curiosity helps us expand and explore possibilities. Genuine, unplanned, unprogrammed response comes from seeing what is in front of us with fresh eyes. We naturally have this innocent, wonder-infused approach to life as children. As we grow up, we start to rely on the reassurance of credentials and expertise, and we can become less open to the discovery available in each new experience. In embracing not-knowing, we become childlike again with awe and reverence for untapped potential. We delight in the dance of possibilities that not-knowing presents.

In school, we are taught that we are supposed to know, and if we don't know, we should at least pretend to know. I remember sitting in business school lectures on days that I had not prepared the case study — I would try to be as inconspicuous as possible while exuding an air of nonchalance. Meanwhile, I was terrified the professor would call on me. If pressed, I would fake my way through. Admitting that I didn't know the answer seemed impossible.

Yet there are benefits to inner dialogue with the space for "I don't know," or "I am curious," or "I wonder if." These hallmarks of the beginner's mind make space for possibility and creativity. When we approach a situation armed with our assumptions or prejudices, we frequently get things wrong. A *don't know* mind provides a role for intuition. A *don't know* mind allows white space for invention. A *don't know* mind gives room for imagination to play. Saying *I don't know* helps us stay present. We can take action to respond to situations in the moment, instead of reacting automatically based on past experience or an imagined future.

Curiosity is the interface layer of Responsiveness, where our inner freedom touches the outer space that opens up for us to play in. When we stop beating ourselves up for not having the answer, we start to celebrate the richness of possibilities present in uncertainty. We become more open-minded in questioning how we are relating to the world. This state of wonder brings presence to the way we respond.

Playfulness (Responsiveness: outer layer)

Playfulness is the public face of Responsiveness. It is the layer where this quality is expressed in the outside world. As children, we are naturally creative because we are naturally playful. At a young age, we haven't yet learned to judge ourselves, our creations, or our efforts, as being good or bad. According to developmental psychology, the concept of competence and performance forms somewhere between the ages of 7 and 11.

Before the point when we start worrying about performing, we are just playing.

Playfulness is about trying things on, or trying things out — without being so concerned about being perfect or polished. It's the temporary suspension of the inner judge that lets us show up without such heavy pressure to perform.

When I first announced to my friends and family that I was going to start writing a book, I shared a memory of the day my three-year-old niece was reading her "book" to me.

My niece's so-called book was a folded piece of paper with a few marker scribbles on it. She held it up proudly and pointed to the page as she read me her story. There were no words on the page. There were no recognizable shapes. It was just an assortment of random squiggles and zigzags. She had such a lively story to tell. It wasn't in complete sentences. It lacked any logical sequence. It definitely didn't have clear subjects and objects. Honestly, it didn't really make a whole lot of sense.

Yet, I nodded and smiled and laughed along with her as she told her story. When she finished her reading, I hugged her and said, "What a wonderful story!"

I reflected on how powerful it would be if I could be that loving and non-judgmental towards myself, as if I were holding my three-year-old self.

What if I celebrated my own story, seeing beauty and experiencing joy in the absolute miracle of pure expression? What if I released the need for this book to be good or be recognized or even be received by anyone? What if I believed that the process itself is enough of an outcome?

When we play, we move with a lightness that is less attached to an outcome. This is the frequency we want to invite if we want to truly respond to life, instead of just reacting to it. When we own our ability to choose, open to the unknown potential inherent in life, and experiment with reality with a sense of playfulness, we are growing in Responsiveness.

Layers of Receptivity

There are three postures that support us in cultivating the quality of Receptivity, as it spirals inward, integrating from our outer reality into our inner being. The three layers of this quality are: humility, fluidity, and worthiness.

- *Humility* (outer layer) is the acknowledgement of where we have needs, which signals our readiness to receive: "I welcome the world's support and guidance."
- *Fluidity* (interface layer) is the embodiment of flexibility and adaptability at the point of contact with the world: "I am willing to be influenced by the world."
- *Worthiness* (inner layer) is the integrated recognition of our inherent value: "I am worthy to receive."

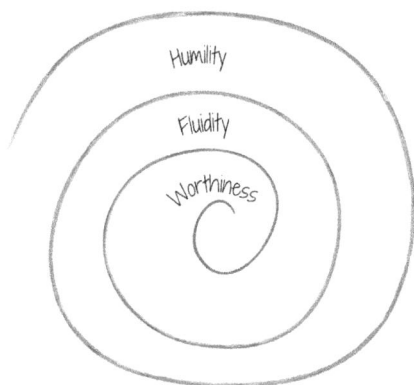

Humility (Receptivity: outer layer)

Humility is the outermost layer of Receptivity. This is where the ability to receive begins, starting from the outside going in. To be able to receive, we must first honor our own needs. This can be a challenge because we are used to presenting ourselves as strong and self-sufficient. We are largely conditioned to hide or disown our needs. In our culture, we like to focus more on our strengths. Being seen as "needy" is often thought of as a sign of weakness or a marker of defect. "Never let them see you sweat" is a common refrain.

Yet we can all use a little help from our friends. The truth is, we all need each other — not only to thrive, but to survive. That help might come in the form of material and financial resources, or in terms of emotional and energetic support. The false idol of independence has deepened our separation from nature and our separation from other human beings. That is why we may feel starved for community.

No human is an island. The idea that we can do everything by ourselves and for ourselves is not only deceptive, it's downright dangerous for humanity. We are all inextricably tied to each other. Forgetting that we are interconnected contributes to exploitative economics built on the false premise of perpetual growth. The myth of separation is what makes billionaires believe they can wait out the apocalypse in their luxury bunkers while the rest of the world burns. But what kind of new world will those billionaires emerge to when the air clears?

Acknowledging our needs creates space for receiving. When we are consumed with trying to seem invincible, we become invisible to those who want to give to us. The idea that one can perpetually gain while others lose is false. Welcoming and recognizing the gifts we receive from others is also a way of giving. We give as we receive when we appreciate, recognize, and reward others for their contributions.

To cultivate Receptivity, we must be humble enough to acknowledge that we need each other, and that needing each other is not a bad thing. Humility is the outer representation of Receptivity. By abiding in humble gratitude, we broadcast to those around us that we are open and ready to receive.

Fluidity (Receptivity: interface layer)

Fluidity is the interface layer of Receptivity, where the outer world comes to shake up our inner world. This is the friction point of this quality. Receptivity is about receiving everything that life has to offer, not just the parts that we personally like or want. Being able to receive also means being open to uninvited feedback, being permeable to unexpected influence, and being flexible with unplanned change. If we are receptive, we are not rigid. Receptivity asks us to be fluid, to "be like water."

Fluidity is called for when we notice attachment to the specific form of what we receive. We may have ideas around the amount of earnings that we want at our new job. We may have ideas around the pedigrees of the participants we prefer to have at our next conference. We may have ideas around the age or profession of the partner that we desire. Consciously or unconsciously, we hold expectations around the things we want to receive; we may even feel that we deserve them or that we have earned them. But what happens sometimes is that while we're looking out the front door waiting for an expected delivery, a surprise gift flies in through the window behind us. Fluidity means being nimble enough to pivot and catch the gift that flies in from nowhere.

Assuming a posture of fluidity also applies to our ability to receive signals. We heartily welcome some signals with ease — they are encouraging; affirming that we are going the right way. At other times, the signals we get are unwelcome. We might receive a rejection that points us in a different direction. We might receive feedback from our audience that what we offer is no longer needed, or not needed in its current form. This can be hard to hear. If we are too attached to our creation, we may block this information from reaching us, or ignore it when it does come through. But the fluidity layer of Receptivity teaches us to allow even unwelcome information. Even if our ego resists it, we can let it in and leverage it. Fluidity helps us switch lanes as life is changing and realign with purpose flow.

Two years ago, I was stressed out, struggling to enroll participants in my women's retreat. I was puzzled because I had offered this retreat several times and it had always filled quite easily before. I was learning to find the edge between letting go and giving up. Here is my self-reflection from that time (taken from a personal blog post):

I have created this thing: a one-week retreat experience for women who want to align with their purpose work. It is a thing that lives outside of me now, having birthed it. But even now, as I prepare to share it again, it keeps teaching me new lessons. I am trying to navigate this space between giving up and letting go. For some mysterious reason, people have been slow to commit to my retreat this time around, and cancellations keep coming. It is so confusing and so disheartening. It has made me question why I even bother. Is this really needed? Am I doing the right things?

I guess that there are no easy answers. I know the way this episode fits into the story of my life won't become clear until later. What can I do? All I know how to do is to use my tools and come back to the only persistent truth: I don't know. I don't know why it suddenly feels harder. I don't know why I've had so many technical difficulties, so many communication challenges, so many unexpected delays. I don't know. I don't know.

What I do know is that giving up is not an option. Giving up means shrinking back and keeping myself small, retreating in fear when I meet resistance, taking my ball and going home when no one wants to play. I am not giving up. I will continue to share, to speak, to give. Even when it feels like I'm standing in an empty room. But I remain open to asking hard questions; open to receiving answers I may not like; and open to change. I am not giving up. This is what I know for sure.

At the same time, I know that letting go is absolutely

required. Letting go means allowing my work to come alive through me, instead of working myself to death by pushing for something. Letting go means staying out of things that are none of my business — like the outcome of my actions. It means acknowledging that ultimately, I have no control over what happens after I do my part by showing up. It means remembering my real work is to keep realigning myself over and over again, and to take action from there.

I am letting go. I am not giving up. This is another opportunity for me to trust more deeply and surrender to something beyond me.

While this was not fun for me at the time, now with 20/20 hindsight I can say that going through this process gave me valuable information. It created a moment of pause in what I had been doing for a while, what had become routine. It caused me to stop, reflect, and turn toward what was to come next — writing this book. Fluidity is an important part of Receptivity. We are always creating concepts and forms around our purpose work. Sometimes we can get fixed or stuck in this. When the feedback and support that we receive from the world creates some conflict with our concepts and forms, then it is time to pause and reconsider our orientation.

Fluidity is the interface layer of Receptivity, where outer and inner worlds collide and create friction. Here, what the world actually presents to us can rub against our overly fixed, pre-existing concepts. Here, the things we are receiving may challenge us to reconsider what we are requesting from the world. This is also the sweet spot where being flexible and adaptable can bring immense rewards.

Worthiness (Receptivity: inner layer)

Worthiness is the innermost layer of Receptivity, where this quality is integrated into our inner being. Receiving requires us to feel worthy of what the world has in store for us. We must believe that we are worthy to receive all the financial resource, emotional support, synchronistic signs, and divine guidance that comes to us. If we are wobbly in our worthiness, we will feel unsure or ungrounded in receiving. When we don't value ourselves enough, we will be blind to — or even block — the gifts that come our way. Building up our Receptivity muscles means training and strengthening our self-worth.

This sense of worth is different from feeling *deserving*. It is not about demanding compensation for the work we are doing. It is not an entitlement card that we trade in for rich rewards. This deep sense of worthiness is not based on credits we have accumulated or merits we have earned. Worthiness naturally emanates from knowing that our human expression is worthy of love, support, and guidance — no matter what. It is a serene and self-less sort of receiving. We simply surrender to our worthiness to receive as we recognize the beauty of our being.

At first glance, worthiness might seem to be the opposite of humility. When we reach a deeper understanding, however, we see that there is no conflict. Worthiness is not competence, and humility is not weakness. We are worthy to receive, no matter who we are — it doesn't matter whether we are good and smart and capable, or not. In humility, we recognize our reliance on the rest of the world without seeing ourselves as deficient in any way. Both worthiness and humility point to our unique value within the web of interdependence that binds us all, while the layer of fluidity allows us to express our unique movements in a dance with our broader family and community.

For many, it is easier to give than to receive. I myself am one of those people who tends to fall out of balance by over-giving and under-receiving. Maybe giving is easier because it assumes a one-up position of strength or superiority. Receiving, on the other hand, may be mistaken as a one-down position of weakness or inferiority. Yet when we are truly standing in our inner-sourced power we can receive like kings and queens without ever feeling diminished in our sense of self-worth. If anything, the cultivation of Receptivity elevates us.

Worthiness is the innermost layer of Receptivity. This is the layer where this quality becomes a part of us. We welcome the abundance that is available. We take to heart all the gifts that the world is always giving to us. We bring these gifts into our center and we allow them to charge us up.

CHAPTER 6

Clearing Space and Making Decisions

The glorification of busy will destroy us.
Without space for healing, without time for reflection,
without an opportunity to surrender, we risk a
complete disconnect from the authentic self.
We burn out on the fuels of willfulness, and eventually
cannot find our way back to center.
— **Jeff Brown**

Purpose is a window that frames how we interpret and interact with reality; how we live our lives. That window has always been there and will always be there. Maybe the window was hidden behind a bookcase for many years and maybe the window was not always clean and clear, but it has always been there. We only need to pay some loving attention to this window to be able to see beauty through it.

I do my best to live my life "on purpose," but there are moments when I'm too tired to resist the pull of conditioning and then my old habits, impulses, and patterns overtake me. That is totally okay. In fact, it is totally expected. I don't need to be on purpose all the time. Losing the way at times is part of the human experience. Purpose guides us to use our time and energy more wisely. It gives us a reason to say "no" to things that are easy and familiar, and a reason to say "yes" to things that are challenging or uncomfortable. But purpose is not here to judge us when we falter. It is normal to stumble along the way. We feel in the flow. We fall out of it. We follow the path. We lose track of it. We just keep coming back to purpose again and again. Purpose serves as a rail that we can use to steady us — it's not meant to be a rule that stifles us.

There are many tools we can use to deepen our qualities of Authenticity, Attunement, Responsiveness, and Receptivity. I share a number of these in the appendix on purpose practices. But let's watch out for the urge to raid the toolshed and haul out as many tools as we can carry. If you feel an itch to get started on your purpose alignment self-improvement project, please relax. Purpose is actually itching to be expressed through us. We don't have to work so hard to make it happen.

We invite the flow of regenerative purpose with two basic orientations in daily life. We demonstrate dedication in space clearing, and we express devotion in decision making. Basically, as much as possible, we want to: (1) keep our personal space clean and clear for creative emergence; and (2) make aligned decisions that direct resources according to our values.

Dedicated space clearing

Time and space are two dimensions in which life happens. We have traditionally been more focused on controlling the use of our time, rather than respecting the power of space. There are stacks of books about how to get things done. We are trained in strategies for efficient time management. We have so many tips and tricks for sorting, scheduling, and tracking tasks. The time focus is sensible when we treat humans as predictable, reliable, independent operators of body-machines. Yet when we view humans as participants in the higher plan of nature, we notice that there's something off about this obsession with time. When we remember that human value goes beyond the checklists we complete, the magic of synchronicity starts to be revered as much as the mastery of productivity. Maintaining space becomes just as important as managing time.

In modern life, "busy" has become a badge of honor. Maybe we make ourselves busy because it gives us some sense of status or importance. Maybe we get busy because it distracts us from the boredom or loneliness within. But when we are busy, we are not available for purpose. Purpose needs space to flow.

When we are busy, instead of being grounded and centered in our true self, we put our ego up front. We make ourselves the hub for information, the bottleneck for action, or the gatekeeper for approval. Things that could be easily handled or quickly passed along to others are slowed down or stopped. We might even subconsciously create some kind of mini-drama around us just to highlight our importance in the story. Our ego is puffed up and put in the way of flow. Our ego obstructs movement because it wants its "there"-ness to be recognized. Stress is a strategy to reinforce the solidity of the egoic self.

To welcome purpose flow, we want to get rid of busy-ness and generate more spaciousness. Having white space in our lives is what gives new ideas, new projects, and new opportunities room to enter. When we are busy, all of the space is taken up. When we are spacious, we clear the way for the movement of life. We make ourselves more available to take part in what is flowing. This is how we interrupt stress circuits and encourage ease. If we want to make room for creative emergence, we need reliable fences and regular garbage removal in our energetic, mental, emotional, and physical spaces.

Energetic space clearing

Energetic space management means paying attention to where we source energy and where we spend energy. When it comes to our personal energy, food, sex, and finances are the big three. Most of us have challenges with the flow of energy in at least one of these three domains — if not all of them. In essence, we need to be attentive to blockages, distortions, or buildup of debris in these areas. If there is pollution in any of these energy flows, it will negatively impact the quality of our presence.

What kind of food are we eating? How are we using our sexuality? What are our behaviors and beliefs when it comes to managing finances? In this inquiry, we might see how we routinely rely on low-quality energy inputs in some areas. We might notice that we have unhealthy addictions to certain energy sources. We might recognize various ways that we unconsciously leak energy. These bad habits are the things we need to clean up to clear energetic space.

Mental space clearing

Mental space management means decluttering our mind from habitual thought patterns. We examine the concepts we carry around that keep us stuck. We look at the beliefs preventing us from fully engaging with reality. Every once in a while, it's good to check out the thoughts we have running in the background, sort through them, and toss the old, tired ones out.

One exercise that I find useful for mental decluttering is freewriting questions. I take out my journal, set a timer for ten minutes, and write one question, then another question, then another question. I continue to write questions repeatedly until the time is up. The key to this practice is to keep going without pausing to consider or answer or edit any of the questions along the way. It's a raw brain dump. This is a quick way to clear mental space, by getting rid of some of the subconscious concerns and worries cluttering our mind.

Emotional space clearing

Emotional space management means inviting the movement of unexpressed emotions, and on a deeper level, holding space for unhealed trauma. We usually notice our emotional clutter piling up in the form of wound narratives, which contribute to habitual feelings and recurring dramas. Since this emotional junk is accumulated in patterns of relating with others, it can be helpful to clean it up in the context of relationship. Any intentional relational field, whether it's with a partner, or friend, or a trained therapist, can support us in emotional space management.

In addition to doing the deep cleaning of deleting old wound narratives, we also need to tidy up our emotional space on a regular basis. We can do that on our own or in the presence of other people, simply by allowing emotional expression or emotional release. Emotional debris builds up when we suppress our emotions. Usually, it's the unpleasant emotions that we hold back — fear, shame, sadness, or anger. By giving ourselves permission to let loose, through crying, or screaming, or laughing, we can clear a lot of emotional space.

Physical space clearing

Physical space management means clearing the clutter from our 3D environment. Spring cleaning is a common shared ritual because we know that a routine purge of our possessions is healthy. It helps us feel fresh. It can be nice to clear out storage places such as the basement or the attic. Though personally, I experience a greater impact from clearing spaces that I see every day. I like to refresh high circulation items (such as underwear, bed sheets, and hygiene tools). And I like to audit things that hang out in high traffic places (such as my hand bag, my car's center console, and my top dresser drawer).

The saying "nature abhors a vacuum" comes from Aristotle's observation that when we remove something from its place, the pressure difference invites an immediate reset to a state of equilibrium. In other words, when we take something out of our space — when we donate a piece of furniture or get rid of an old sweater, for example — the absence that that action creates will quickly be filled. When we clear space in our lives, we invite new life to enter in.

According to the Chinese wisdom of *feng shui*, we need to clear space to facilitate the unobstructed flow of *chi*, or life force. Many feng shui practitioners perform a daily ritual of sweeping the area just outside their front door. This is a symbolic act of ushering out old energy and preparing the space to welcome new life. Whether it is mental, emotional, physical, or energetic space, creating space is a sweeping practice. Left unswept, our spaces become cluttered. The structures that grow in these spaces get calcified over time. Our sense of spaciousness is compromised and the flow of energy gets contracted.

Devotional decision making

We can view life as a progression, as we move forward along a linear path. Or we can view life as an expansion, as we take part in an evolutionary dance. As we discussed before, the default mode of the old paradigm usually has us moving towards a goal. We have a destination in mind. We map out a route and make a plan. Then we take a series of steps to get from here to there. We want to force the future to conform to our personal will; this desire is super strong. But regenerative purpose invites us to view life as an organic process that's always unfolding. This new-paradigm view requires us to release the illusion of control.

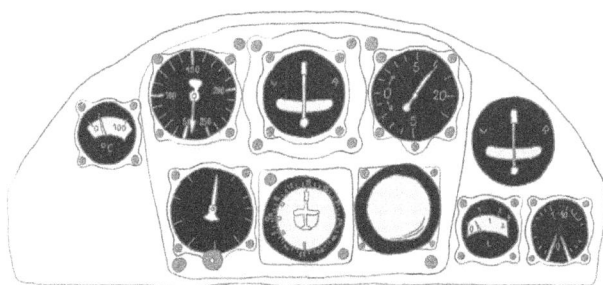

Last year, I learned about the art of flight navigation as I was in a small Cessna flying over the San Francisco Bay with my pilot friend James. I found out that pilots do not fly the airplane in a straight line from point A to point B. Because the wind and weather are so unpredictable, pilots must make tiny course corrections throughout the flight. The aggregate of all those small adjustments eventually takes the plane where it needs to go. This is a beautiful metaphor for how purpose works. A purpose-full life is not about following a straight line to reach an endpoint. Rather it is a winding journey that results from the accumulated impact of daily choices, weekly routines, monthly rituals, and longer-term commitments.

It might be easier to see how this works when we look in the rearview mirror. Ten years ago, I could not have imagined my life as it is today. What matters to me now is completely foreign from what I thought I wanted back then. My current reality wasn't even a possibility that my mind could have grasped at that time. There is no way that that past version of me could have figured out how to get here from there because the old me didn't even know that this "here" existed! Yet when I look backwards at the stepping stones that appeared one by one, the process of arriving where I am now reveals itself as a brilliantly designed plan. It just wasn't *my* plan.

It wasn't my plan, but to be fair, I was not skipping blindly through life either. I made conscious decisions. I was constantly checking in to make sure my choices were aligned with my ethics and values, and with creating the most value. In choosing which way to turn, four questions guided me at every fork in the road:

	Energetic currency (time, attention)	Material currency (money, assets)
...aligned with my core values?	Is the way that I spend my time and attention in alignment with my core values?	Is the way that I spend my money and use my assets in alignment with my core values?
...creating what is most valued?	Am I contributing time and attention in places where I can provide the most value?	Am I investing materially to support myself and others to create what I most value?

The answers to these four questions are rarely obvious. We usually need to zoom out to be able to see how our choices impact our reality. We need to step back to encompass a broader worldview, or we need to step up to envision a longer time span. These four questions can be summarized in one broad inquiry to support day-to-day devotional decision making, which is: *Am I stewarding resources towards creating what I value?*

Purpose is the sacred union of a divine plan and grounded action. As human lightning rods, we are made to grab ethereal concepts and ideals and translate them into practical, tangible reality. We are doing this all the time, whether we realize it or not. We shape the outer world and we create our inner reality with the resources we have at hand. How we choose to spend and invest our energetic and material currency is ultimately how we choose to deploy our life force.

While a momentary crisis might motivate a single, symbolic, visible action — such as walking in a protest march, signing a petition, or collecting donations for a cause — it is the accumulated impact of our collective, repetitive, daily decisions that create the biggest waves of change. We express our values and assign value with the seemingly small choices we make every single day. Making these day-to-day decisions intentionally, with devotion, is what unleashes purpose flow.

Our values help us decide what to do, where to move. They clarify our preferences and priorities. In some moments, we may deviate from the guidance of our values compass because we are pressed to make compromises — for convenience, safety, or financial necessity. We make temporary sacrifices to build resilience or gather resources for the road ahead. Yet being purpose-aligned means we are vigilant in consciously minding how we spend our time, attention, money, and other resources.

Voting with our time

We vote for the kind of world we want to live in with our time. When I pressed the "eject" button on my consulting career to launch myself into the scary unknown, that decision was motivated by a mismatch in values. I loved the freedom of working remotely. But I didn't love the long hours and weekend work. I loved the camaraderie and connection that I had with my colleagues and clients. But I didn't love working for multinational corporations in financial services or oil and gas. I felt depleted because my time was enlisted to support misaligned missions. I was spending my time in ways that were inconsistent with — or even contrary to — my values.

My consulting role was also misaligned because I was not growing and evolving in it. In some ways, the work seemed challenging: I was under pressure to perform, on a demanding schedule, and stretched by the intellectual rigor of my work. Yet I was not challenged to expand the expression of my true self. I was not called to tap into my deepest genius. I was not compelled to bring my unique gifts to bear. I was nowhere close to touching my personal evolutionary edge. I was treading water at the shallow end of my potential, trading my time for the comfort of a secure paycheck while clutching the safety blanket of complacency. I realized that it was high time to do something different with my valuable time.

Voting with our attention

In the increasingly digital world we live in, attention is a specific, time-related resource that bears separate mention. Surely, our physical presence casts a vote for the kind of world we want to live in, but so does our virtual presence. Marketers have massive budgets that are earmarked to "pay for clicks" — so it is worth noticing where we are spending our attention currency. What sources do we rely on for our news? What shows do we watch? What influencers do we follow? What apps do we use on our smart phone? Are the individuals and institutions that we patronize with our attention actually aligned with our values? Looking into this is the start of a purpose-full shift. Simply by attending to where our attention goes, and becoming aware of who or what is benefiting from that attention, we can already effect huge changes.

We can play an important role in directing others' attention to causes and companies that we care about. We each have a platform to communicate and share what we value with our social circles. It doesn't matter whether that is a circle of one million people, or one dozen. If there is a small business in your community that has an ecological ethic that excites you, you can write them a review. If there is a social justice columnist whose essays inspire you, you can share their writing on social media. We direct attention currency by signal boosting those who are doing things that we value. This is part of our purpose work.

Voting with our money

Of course, we also shape the world with the ways we spend money and other material resources. Making value-based choices means assigning value in the outer world according to our inner values. It means redirecting resources in the physical realm to reflect priorities that come from the emotional, moral, and spiritual realms. This means casting votes with our wallets on a daily basis, which can be even more powerful than casting votes with ballots. Collectively, our buying decisions are investments in change. Our money and material resources are vehicles for transformation.

Two summers ago, I met Irena Ateljevic, founder of Sibenik Hub for Ecology, while traveling in Croatia. Irena was a pioneer in establishing the first organic vegan cafe in her city. Driven by purpose, she made a conscious decision to source produce from local farmers instead of from global grocery conglomerates. As a result of this choice, customers often complain that her prices are too high. Most of them have no idea how much thinner her profit margins are compared to those of a traditional restaurant using imported and processed ingredients. Instead of seeing this as a loss, she accepts lower margins as an investment in what she values. Her values-based decision generates less profit for her in the short-term, but creates what she values in the long-term.

In the purpose world, teachers and leaders often say: "Do what you love and the money will come." With this, we acknowledge that there is an expected time gap between sharing our purpose offering to the world, and then at some point later, being valued for this offering and supported to continue. Doing what we love and waiting for the money to come requires patience, persistence, and yes, also privilege. The amount of trust we can afford to help us bridge that time-gap is highly correlated with the amount of privilege we enjoy.

It is not surprising that many purpose workers struggle to be paid well, because we don't yet live in a world that values and rewards this kind of work. A lot of self-help directs us to examine our money stories and internalized beliefs around self-worth, but this is not something that can be solved purely with personal development. We also have to look at institutionalized injustices before we can truly change the paradigm. We suffer from patriarchy, oligarchy, racism, sexism, classism, and many other kinds of kyriarchy. These old-paradigm power structures are systems defined by the domination of an elite few. Personal development work alone is not sufficient to birth the New Earth. Collectively, we also need to change the water we swim in. We need to transform structures and systems by changing how we exchange value with each other.

If we want to get paid well for purpose work, the fastest road to that future is to be zealous and generous in paying others for their purpose work. As a society, we pay Facebook executives and football players an absolute fortune. We leak so much energy to these individuals — billions of dollars and trillions of hours. Imagine the changes that we would see if everyone made paying for contributions to humanity's collective evolution a higher priority than paying for the creation of mass distraction.

When we look closely at where we spend money, where do we see our financial power going? Can we spend less money on unnecessary objects and mindless entertainment? Is there room to invest a bit more in local economic ecosystems? Are there resources that can be used to promote and support the purpose pioneers who are creating, serving, leading, and teaching in our neighborhoods and communities?

It is tempting to point the finger at others and judge them as less evolved because they don't value what we value. But we each need to look within, and start the change with our own choices. To feel valued for being aligned with our values, we need to share value with those who are aligned with our values. We make default decisions to allocate economic value all the time, without ever considering what that energy is supporting. Becoming more aware of this is how we can create values-based economic ecosystems around everything that we buy, supply, trade, consume, and use. We give resources to individuals and businesses that resonate with our belief system. We pay for work that is consistent with our core principles. The network effect can spread this ethos — and the accompanying economic impact — organically and quickly. By voting with our money, we move to make material value match our moral values.

The declaration of purpose

Now, if living on purpose is simply about clearing space and making aligned decisions on a day-to-day basis, is there anything that is evergreen about our purpose? How do we codify our purpose? How do we claim it? How do we commit to it?

It is a common coaching exercise to craft a purpose statement — a sentence or two that summarizes your personal mission. It is an "elevator pitch" explanation for your existence. It is a catchphrase that is usually short and sometimes inspirational. It is a declaration that describes your "why."

Here are a few examples of typical purpose statements:

My purpose is...
- To enable others to express more of their true selves
- To help people embrace healthy risks without fear
- To support flourishing, healthy, mature relationships
- To inspire positive change through teaching and coaching
- To empower other women in greater sexual freedom
- To create growth opportunities for young adults
- To bridge understanding as a speaker and writer
- To support others to identify their gifts and talents

These purpose statements share some common themes. They all reflect a desire to make use of a personal strength to be of service to a particular group of people. They all demonstrate a motivation to help others, to make a positive impact, or to contribute to creating a better world. Most people reading these statements would nod at the nobility of these causes.

These kinds of statements are useful personal touchstones. They remind us to stay focused on the impact we want to have, or rally us to persist through challenges. They help us find our way back to the path when we get lost. They can also make lovely branding messages for purpose-powered products and services. If we leave it there though, we run the risk of experiencing purpose that is only skin deep, not soul deep.

Make commitments, not statements

For soul-deep purpose, we have to make and honor purpose-based commitments. As sweet as they may sound, purpose statements are not that useful when it comes to actually living our purpose. In our efforts to free up space and make good decisions on a day-to-day basis, these inspirational boilerplates will not help us. Such declarations do nothing to open and conduct the flow of purpose. We need something else to support purpose alignment in everyday life. Beyond the boilerplate, what we need are clear commitments that set firm boundaries and guide principled choices.

Two kinds of commitments help facilitate purpose flow:

1. *Selection-commitments* are the commitments that support dedicated space clearing by defining our boundaries.

2. *Direction-commitments* are the commitments that support devotional decision-making by guiding our choices.

Selection commitments

Selection commitments mark our boundary edges. They help us draw a bright line between the people, things, and experiences we want to include in our lives and those we want to exclude.

The diva of decluttering, Marie Kondo, has popularized her filter for getting rid of unnecessary objects: Does it spark joy? She suggests tossing out things that do not spark joy when we touch them. This rule is simplistic but it's a good example of a filter that is used to select what we allow into our space. It determines what is in and what is out. It tells us what is allowed through the front gate as things come to us. It tells us what goes out with the trash when things are ready to leave us.

Some examples of selection-commitments are:

- I commit to only accepting Facebook friend requests from people whom I have met at least once in real life
- I commit to donating any clothing items that I haven't worn in more than a year

- I commit to ceasing my efforts to connect with friends when they do not reciprocate for one month

Direction commitments

Direction-commitments guide our actions. They are principles that help us decide which way to go when we are at a crossroads. They tell us when to turn left; when to turn right; and when to make a U-turn and go back the way we came.

Direction-commitments clarify the foundational values that act as guardians of our choices. They serve as guiding principles that we can fall back on when we have difficult decisions to make. These commitments can be expressed as priorities or preferences. They make it obvious when one choice is more aligned with our values than another. These kinds of direction-commitments help us choose between options by clarifying the reason for taking this path over that path.

Some examples of direction-commitments are:
- I commit to choosing to work with organizations based on my alignment with their mission and values
- I commit to buying organic produce from the farmers' market instead of the nearest global chain grocery
- I commit to patronizing restaurants that are locally owned and managed over international brands

Ultimately, the purpose statements that we craft to declare our life's mission to the world often end up being largely for appearance's sake. On the other hand, when we make purpose-full commitments, we put in a grounding stake.

CHAPTER 7

The Regenerative Nature of Purpose

When we can truly see and understand the Earth,
love is born in our hearts. We feel connected.
That is the meaning of love: to be at one. Only
when we've truly fallen back in love with the
Earth will our actions spring from reverence
and the insight of our interconnectedness.
— **Thich Nhat Hanh**

We use the word "regenerative" to refer to something that is reborn or restored to a higher state. This is becoming a popular term among scientists, activists, and educators who are restoring ecosystems and developing ecological resilience. Regenerative consciousness culture emphasizes the transformational power of natural cycles. In contrast, the old-paradigm, goal-obsessed, objectification of purpose is ecologically blind. Stepping into the new paradigm of regenerative purpose means working with purpose in a way that respects and mirrors the laws of nature.

Scientific and technological advances have significantly increased overall levels of security, prosperity, and health over the past 500 years. Unfortunately, while we humans were making ourselves at home on Earth, we also became parasites to our planetary host. Consumerism has led us to rob collective resources in order to turn plunder into profit for an elite few. Because of our separation from nature, the planet is sick and we are sick. The consequences of our exploitative relationship with nature are painfully apparent in the form of climate and ecological crisis; physical and mental health disintegration; and social, political, and economic instability.

Sustainability professor Glenn Albrecht has even coined a term for the negative mental health impact of humanity's disconnection from nature; he calls it *psychoterratic*. Along the same lines, cell biologist Bruce Lipton offers another striking metaphor for our current dilemma: "When the cells in our bodies fight one another, we call that autoimmune disease. What humanity, the superorganism comprising seven billion people on this planet, is experiencing now is a very bad case of autoimmune disease."

Regenerative purpose is medicine for this malaise. It is a way of working that follows natural rhythms, seasons, and cycles. It finds a healthy balance between being and doing. It includes both inner work and outer work. It bridges spiritual connection and grounded collaboration. It unleashes the magical powers of human creation without disrespecting the matching powers of destruction. Humans have shown a tendency to want to conquer and contain nature in the pursuit of unchecked, limitless growth. Now as we see the pendulum swinging back in the opposite direction, we must learn to surrender to nature's rhythms and honor the completion of cycles in death.

The purpose trap

In the beginning, we may hesitate to engage in serious inquiry about why we are here or how we are meant to serve. The purpose question is daunting. It can feel too abstract or too big. Even if the answer came, we might worry: *If I find out about purpose, what could that possibly mean for how I choose to live my life? What might I have to give up? What might I have to risk? What might I have to try?* The weight of these questions can keep us from exploring. We avoid or delay getting intimate with purpose because we know that we are not yet ready to do what will be required once we connect to it with clarity.

At the other end of the purpose life cycle, our purpose has usually gotten tangled up with our identity and public image. We have formed a self-concept around our purpose form — it is imprinted on business cards, websites, or social media. We have probably invested a lot of energy into creating a program, a product, a service, or an entire business. With all the effort that we put into building this purpose form, it can be hard to let go, if it turns out that letting go is what is needed. Attachment to our creation can cause us to get stuck in one instance of purpose expression, which slows down or stops its natural evolution. The idea that "I have found my purpose" or "I have figured out my purpose" actually disconnects us from the life energy of purpose flow. We pass by present opportunities to grow and expand when we are too comfortable resting on past achievements.

The traditional view of purpose is limiting in two ways: It can prevent us from getting started at the beginning of the purpose life cycle, and it can prevent us from letting go of a particular purpose expression long after its expiration date. Whether we are stuck in not realizing it or stuck in not releasing it, both traps block us from fully participating in the flow of purpose. The point of purpose is not to achieve "purpose-having" status. The point of purpose is to access a state of activation that brings us into full, ecstatic, embodied engagement with life. We cannot capture purpose and put it in a box. If we somehow manage to do this, then what happens is that purpose ends up putting *us* in a box, where we will stagnate if we stay. When we are too attached to the purpose form, it becomes limiting rather than liberating.

Regenerative purpose is fluid and ever-changing. It asks us to drop the idea of purpose as an identity-defining concept. Instead it invites us to engage with purpose in co-creative conversation. Purpose is our natural way of living when we are in love with life. First, we must recognize purpose as a force of nature, and remember ourselves as part of that nature. From there, we can see how the form of purpose is impermanent and the essence of purpose is interdependent.

Balance between being and doing

In fast-moving modern life, we tend to focus on what we are doing and moving in the world because it is obvious from outside. The scientific mind loves to track, explain, and predict and measure what we can observe. The state of our being, on the other hand, is internal and invisible. We discount the impact of stillness because it's not apparent to the eye. We have to call on other senses to bring forth the value of the unseen.

Yet when we remember that we are an expression of nature, we remember that being and doing are both essential to life. Nature is marked by cycles of moving and resting, waking and sleeping, eating and digesting, being and doing. The way nature *is* cannot be less important than what nature *does*. Aligning with nature calls for us to return to this balance.

Authenticity and Attunement — the qualities of being —

bring perspective and intention. These "being qualities" help us clear space for the emergence of truth as we rest, reflect, and connect. Responsiveness and Receptivity — the qualities of doing — bring balance and integrity. These "doing qualities" help us stay aligned as we engage, create, and serve.

When we overemphasize the qualities of being, we suffer stagnation. We may feel peaceful, but we can get frustrated over what is left unrealized. Without enough doing, we shortchange the impact that is possible. On the other hand, when we overemphasize the qualities of doing, we suffer burnout. We may feel powerful, but we can get overwhelmed as our activity becomes unsustainable. Without enough being, our actions are not sourced from a deeper well.

When we find the right balance of being and doing, we experience richness and fullness in our lives. We see tangible effects from periods of intentional non-doing. And when we move, we move with a heightened sense of presence. As we develop the four core purpose qualities, our reality starts to feel less busy and more easy. The visible forms and structures of our lives may or may not change. Either way, the shift in us will be hard for others to pinpoint. This unnamable difference is the embodied experience of inner-sourced, regenerative purpose.

The problem with perpetual growth

One of the major reasons that humans have made a mess on this planet is the myth of perpetual growth. There is a cosmic law that tells us the universe is always expanding. However, this expansion is happening on the quantum level beyond physical form. In physical reality, healthy, creative, generative life forms do not grow linearly and limitlessly. The perpetual growth that humans are addicted to is unnatural. In nature, when life exhibits unchecked growth, it is a disease; it is a virus; it is cancer.

From a spiritual point of view, source or essence is pure potential. This essence encompasses endless possibilities and exists free from limitations. But the material world is limited. In a finite, three-dimensional reality, something cannot come from nothing without a cost. Under the enchantment of perpetual growth addiction, we just ignore this reality by hiding the cost.

In *Sacred Economics,* Charles Eisenstein explains how interest-based loans (the technical term is usury) embedded perpetual growth into our global financial systems. "Because of interest, at any given time the amount of money owed is greater than the amount of money already existing. To keep the system going, we have to create more goods and services." He offers a standard recipe for getting rich in this system: "Find anything that people do for themselves or do for each other for free. Then take it away from them: make it illegal, inconvenient, or otherwise unavailable. Then sell back to them what you have taken."

With a system that relies on perpetual growth, we are forced to create something from nothing. This is a problem, because the only way that we can grow wealth infinitely in a limited physical world is if we grab free shared resources and turn them into private property. We take what is "ours" and make it "mine" in order to turn a profit. We cut rain forests into lumber. We tap mountain springs to bottle drinking water. We turn social reciprocity (for things like massage, or childcare) into paid professional services. The elite have done this for ages: assumed ownership of nature's assets to package them and sell them back to the masses. Sadly, there are huge hidden costs baked into the perpetual growth economy. It weakens community, wastes resources, and contaminates common spaces.

With growing ecological awareness, we have started to shift from obsessive growth to a sustainability ethos. Many are trying to slow down the extraction of virgin resources, while others are educating people about the polluting impact of disposable plastic products. As fashion journalist Alexander Fury notes, "We can't continue to produce product incessantly, and believe that there is infinite market — and simply, room — for everything we manufacture and then discard." The growing awareness around this is a good start, but still, we need to move from a sustainability ethos to a regenerative culture.

Earlier this year, I wrote a Facebook post about the ecological impact of burning *palo santo* wood. I shared that these trees are considered endangered in two countries and suggested that people not buy the wood because this contributes to widening the pool of global demand that encourages illegal logging of these trees. That post went somewhat viral.

The owner of a business that is a well-known purveyor of palo santo was one of the people who responded ardently to my post. He wanted me to know that the wood he sells is certified "sustainable" because it is only harvested from deadwood trees. He argued that hypothetically even if we burned up all the deadwood that exists, there would still be plenty of living trees. Months later, he continued to send me articles on the distinctions between subspecies of trees, eager to prove that the trees he harvests from are not technically endangered (yet).

This highlighted the limitations of a sustainability mindset for me. The average lifespan of a palo santo tree is 40-50 years for female trees and up to 200 years for male trees. If I planted a palo santo tree today, it is unlikely that I would see it grow to maturity, die naturally, and rest on the forest floor long enough to be ethically harvested according to local shamanic tradition. I guess it is nice to know that some palo santo comes from trees that officially died of natural causes. But what is more important for me is knowing that my buying choices are not contributing to global market demand for Amazonian hardwoods. Even if my purchase is certified sustainable, buying *any* palo santo adds to the growing economic incentive to harvest a limited resource — a hardwood that humans are capable of consuming much faster than nature is producing.

To move to a regenerative mindset, we have to stop congratulating ourselves for merely slowing down the race of resource extraction. We have to focus on planting, nurturing, revitalizing, and reinvesting. It's time to drop out of the toxic competition to maximize what we can get for less. Instead, we must take only what we need, and give back not only what we receive, but more. Striving to give back more than we receive needs to become the new normal. We need to plant more trees than we cut down. We need to create more than we consume. We need to step into loving and supporting each other way beyond what we think is humanly possible.

Moving to a regenerative mindset

When we connect to the experience of living *on* purpose, we are connected to the flow of life. But when we are concerned with finding *a* purpose, we get disconnected. In disconnection, we become susceptible to seeking behavior. When we see purpose as a desirable thing to have, we can get addicted to chasing purpose the same way that we have been addicted to chasing money, status, power, or security.

Being a pioneer in the regenerative purpose paradigm is not easy. It takes courage to do things that fly in the face of current culture. It takes conviction to confront the dysfunctions that have long been considered normal. Most of us have been raised with growth-focused mantras as inspiration or encouragement. We are told to: "go big or go home," "scale or die," "dream bigger," and "never give up." We don't even notice the perpetual growth addiction that is subconsciously woven into these messages. We live in a culture that glorifies big-ness, makes growth the primary goal, and puts persistence on a pedestal. Perpetual growth is part of our default programming.

Modern humans have gotten quite good at rapidly growing and scaling things, but we are shockingly unskilled when it comes to gracefully dying. For example, "growth hacking" is now a popular discipline in the tech world, defined as "the relentless focus on growth as the only metric that truly matters." Within the natural cycle of life, birth and growth are counterbalanced by death and decay. With the pervasiveness of perpetual growth thinking, we have completely lost touch with this basic law of nature.

We build businesses, develop programs, design websites, or write books. We put love, sweat, and tears into creating these purpose forms, and naturally we get attached to them. But we have to remember that the forms we create are impermanent. We may create some purpose forms that outlive us. Other purpose forms may shine for only a brief moment before they collapse into the compost bin. The life span of our purpose form could be ninety years, ninety days, or ninety minutes. With the rapid rate of change we face today, it is more and more common that the purpose life cycles we hold will be shorter than our human life span. This means we need to get better at letting go. No matter how long it lasts, whatever form we create from purpose will eventually die.

The seasons of purpose

The purpose flow model describes a circular movement with four dimensions or four phases, which can be mapped to the seasonal cycles of nature. Nature is constantly going through a process of birth, growth, decay, death, and rebirth. The cycles of regenerative purpose mimic the cycles of nature because they are an expression of nature. As human beings, we are part of nature and purpose is the way we engage with life.

In nature, the change of seasons is marked by different amounts of daylight, different temperatures, different weather, and different levels of activity. Depending on where we live in the world, we see various types and degrees of seasonal shifts. When we look at the dynamic movement of purpose, we see how its flow also follows metaphorical seasons.

There are four phases in the regenerative purpose cycle: incubation, creation, expression, and reflection. These phases are marked by different activities and different qualities, much like the seasons of nature. The four phases of purpose flow can show up for longer or shorter time periods. The phases can also occur simultaneously and overlap each other.

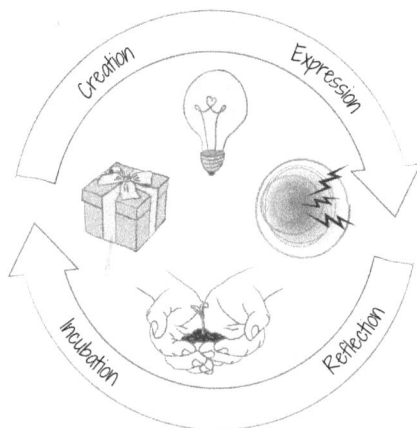

1. *Incubation.* In the winter, we usually stay inside more. We try to conserve our energy as we rest and recharge. Invisible, internal processes of integration and incubation are taking place during this time. We digest our experiences, grounding the useful lessons and getting rid of the useless residue. On the outside, not much is moving. In the purpose flow diagram, this phase takes place where the energy of receiving meets the individual (represented by the GIFT on the left side of the cycle diagram). This is where Abundance Flow enters our personal space. Here we allow resources to restore and replenish our charge.

2. *Creation.* Our energy is expanding when it is springtime. We emerge from hibernation, invigorated after a period of deep rest. We are inspired and motivated. We may experience a burst of forward momentum as we start new projects or set out on new adventures. It is a time for initiation. We begin to step out of our cave and into the world, vibrant and vital. In

the purpose flow diagram, this phase takes place where the individual (GIFT) begins to move towards the collective, with the energy of giving as we respond from presence. This is where the flow of creativity starts moving. Here our authentic gifts begin to be revealed and take shape as purpose forms.

3. *Expression.* During summer, we reach the peak of our external expression. We are highly active, connected, and engaged in what we are doing. This is the phase of purpose flow when we get immersed in creation. We are focused. We are productive. We are generative. We feel like we are "on fire." Our productivity-driven culture tends to prize this phase the most, and for a while, many modern workplaces demanded for us to be in this state all the time. The problem is that when we stay in summer too long, we can get burned out by our own fire — a common affliction in modern life. In the purpose flow diagram, the summer phase is where the energy of giving meets the rest of the world. Here we see how our contribution impacts the collective.

4. *Reflection.* Our energy retreats in the autumn. It is the season for releasing the past. We start to wind down our activity level and withdraw inward. We review and reflect on what we have done and what we have learned. We shed old forms and compost them to provide nourishment for next season's growth. In the purpose flow diagram, this phase takes place where Abundance Flow emanates from the world and moves toward us. Here the world becomes a source of guidance and support for us. We receive feedback from the collective

and we use it to reassess and realign. Depending on what comes to us, we are able to understand what we need to shed and what we need to shift.

We miss out on the vitality of purpose if we imagine that we have reached the pinnacle of purpose and fall asleep there, feeling satisfied. Purpose is more enlivening when we engage in it as a way to open up to all of life — and death is an inescapable part of life. This means honoring the beauty and power of our creations without grasping on to them. It means letting go of projects and roles with grace and humility when it's time to let go. It means purpose-fully destroying what we have built in order to make space for new forms to emerge. We are always creating, always growing, and always dying — all at the same time. To open to the flow of regenerative purpose, we have to lean into death and decay as part of the process.

From empire building to wave making

When we embrace death as part of the purpose process, we naturally start to shift towards making waves, rather than building empires. Empire building is about creating forms, structures, and systems that will outlast us. We are pushed by an egoic desire to leave behind a permanent imprint of our existence — our legacy. Wave making, on the other hand, is not concerned with the identity of the individuals involved. Instead, we are pulled into a movement that is beyond us. We are water droplets in a wave. This wave gains strength and momentum as more of us participate. It has natural ebbs and flows. No single drop directs the wave, but every drop contributes.

The antidote to glorifying big-ness is not shrinking or

withdrawing from the arena. The opposite of "go big or go home" is not "stay small," nor is it "don't bother trying at all." No, that's not it. What we are invited into is the paradox of accessing our immense power, while acknowledging our absolute insignificance. If we can access the space where these seeming contradictions converge, we can say "yes" to empowered and enlivened participation in a purpose-full life as we link arms to make a catalytic collective impact. When we join millions of voices in concert, the sound is deafening, even when no one is screaming. When we reunite with the global family of humanity, our individual actions are amplified to world-changing proportions.

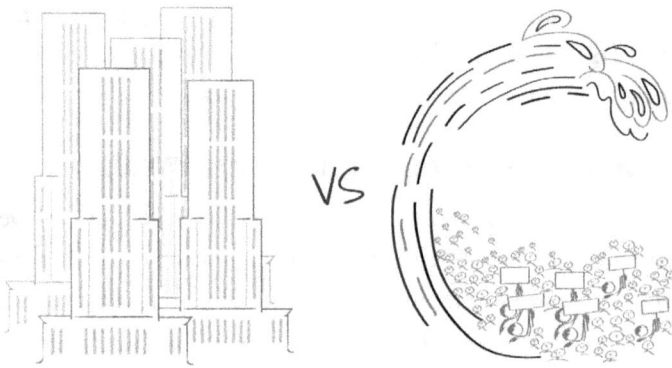

We can reclaim energy that we would otherwise put into building a personal empire to be our ego-shrine. We can relax any anxiety around leaving a legacy behind. We may leave a lasting personal legacy or we may not, but it doesn't matter. Regenerative purpose asks us to examine which waves we choose to amplify instead. Wave making is what happens when we connect to purpose as a force of nature. The collective impulse becomes central and the individual agendas that support that wave become elemental. We understand that we are all valuable, but no one is important. We are all unique, but no one is special. We embrace our insignificance without retreating into ambivalence — this is how we shine in regenerative purpose.

From pushing forward to flowing with

When we drop the ego-activity of building empires and connect with the collective power to make waves instead, we may face resistance from the mind. Most of us have a deeply ingrained habit of wanting to control situations or have mastery over our environment. Even though energy, focus, and motivation do naturally ebb and flow, our go-go-go modern way of life ignores this. Our productivity culture imposes unrealistic demands for us to be "full-on" all the time. Disengaging from that pre-installed program creates dissonance.

As I was writing this book, the theme of not pushing came up again and again. "No pushing" is one of the cardinal school rules that many of us are taught in kindergarten. As it turns out, this is also a lesson for life. This is evidently a lesson that I am still learning. My mind set so many deadlines throughout the book-writing process — for completing chapters; for hiring an illustrator; for submitting the manuscript to my editors. Every time when I had a timeline in mind, I was reminded that the schedule I was following was not actually mine. This book has stubbornly marched to its own rhythm — with many stops and starts. It has come through in its own sweet time.

In the spring of 2019, I received a strong reminder to surrender to a larger plan. This is what I shared about my experience at that time:

I am leaving Thailand in just over a week. I will be moving around a lot for the next month. I thought I was going to have the first draft of my book finished before I started traveling. I was hoping to have it signed, sealed and sent off to my editors before I get on the ferry next Tuesday.

Aggressive goal maybe, but the way things have been flowing it seemed doable. I was pretty close. I have an overall structure. Most of the core content is now in the form of sentences, shaped into paragraphs and written down in Word documents. I only had the introduction and conclusion left to write and about six more interview transcripts to go through and cull for quotes and stories.

In the last few days, I started to feel a bit pressured by this time box that I had put myself in. I noticed myself feeling restless and anxious for the first time since I started the writing process. It's a vaguely familiar feeling to me because it's the way that I used to work, all of the time. It's also a strange feeling to me because it's not how I usually experience work these days.

Feeling that something was off, I started to take inventory of my life. I started going through my mental to-do list of tasks, obligations, events, and appointments. I was looking for places where I could say "no" more. I reflected to a friend that maybe I needed to reconsider my own self-imposed deadline because it's not aligned with my menstrual cycle. Not only am I getting myself ready for transition this week, but also, I'm expecting my period... the worst possible time to be pushing myself to do anything.

Then yesterday I was sitting in a cafe. I wanted to charge both my laptop and my phone... at the same time. I plugged my laptop into the wall and then tried to plug my phone into the USB port of my laptop. It wasn't going in easily. Halfway present with what I was doing, I pushed the phone cable in a little bit harder. Really, I shoved it. And as soon as I succeeded in making that happen, I saw a spark and the laptop stopped charging. The adapter was still attached to my laptop but the light went out. No more power was going in. Now my laptop is completely out of battery and unusable.

Wow. The message couldn't be any clearer to me. This book is not controlled by me. It will come when it wants to come. I have to allow it, not push it. This is one of the messages in the book, which apparently is a lesson that I'm still learning.

The book doesn't care that I am getting on a plane in 8 days. It doesn't give a shit about my travel schedule. It's not important to the book that it would be convenient for me to have a draft finished before I leave. The book isn't concerned with my mind-created timeline. Not at all. It has its own plan, its own process. It seems that I needed to be reminded that I am in service to this book, and not the other way around. Okay. Message received.

There is a funny and somewhat embarrassing end to this story. Weeks later, I discovered that my laptop had not actually died. Only the charger needed to be replaced. That could have been resolved almost immediately, but it took me three weeks to figure out that it was something so easily handled. So, as it turns out, this whole episode with the black screen of death was an illusion. It was a trick of perception, which led me to take a much-needed break when I was pushing too hard.

The success myth of bigger and faster

There are two major success myths that we bump up against when we choose to approach work in a way that aligns with nature. One is the "bigger" myth and the other one is the "faster" myth. The secret is that bigger and faster are not always better. In fact, it's usually the opposite. We have been told that bigger and faster are signposts on the road to success, but on the path of purpose, they are traps. Going after bigger and faster often leads to unnecessary sacrifice, stress, and struggle.

Have you heard the Brazilian folk story about the fisherman and the businessman?

> There was once a businessman who was sitting by the beach in a small Brazilian village. As he sat, he saw a Brazilian fisherman rowing a small boat towards the shore having caught quite a few big fish. The businessman was impressed and asked the fisherman, "How long does it take you to catch so many fish?"
>
> The fisherman replied, "Oh, just a short while."
>
> "Then why don't you stay longer at sea and catch even more?"
>
> "This is enough to feed my whole family," the fisherman said.
>
> The businessman asked, "So, what do you do for the rest

of the day?"

The fisherman replied, "Well, I usually wake up early in the morning, go out to sea and catch a few fish, then go back and play with my kids. In the afternoon, I take a nap with my wife, and evening comes, I join my buddies in the village for a drink — we play guitar, sing and dance throughout the night."

The businessman offered a suggestion to the fisherman. "I have a degree in business management. I can help you to become more successful. From now on, you should spend more time at sea and try to catch as many fish as possible. When you have saved enough money, you could buy a bigger boat and catch even more fish. Soon you will be able to afford to buy more boats, set up your own company, your own production plant for canned food and distribution network. By then, you will have moved out of this village and to Sao Paulo, where you can set up headquarters to manage your other branches."

The fisherman continues, "And after that?"

The businessman laughs heartily, "After that, you can live like a king in your own house, and when the time is right, you can go public and sell your company shares in the stock exchange, and you will be rich."
The fisherman asks, "And after that?"

The businessman says, "After that, you can finally retire, you can move to a house by the fishing village, wake up early in the morning, catch a few fish, then return home to play with kids, have a nice afternoon nap with your wife, and *when evening comes, you can join your buddies for a drink, play the guitar, sing and dance throughout the night!"*

The fisherman was puzzled, "Isn't that what I am doing now?"

I have heard a lot of well-meaning advice about how I could scale my women's retreats (be big!) or how I could expand my biodegradable glitter empire (grow fast!). All this advice comes with good intentions and a desire to see me "succeed," but I think it misses the point. In my view, success means that I can consciously choose what I do with my money, time, attention, and other resources, and I get to vote for the kind of world that I want to see with those choices.

When small is better than big

Years ago, I read a post from leadership coach Nisha Moodley where she discussed her decision to keep her women's retreats small. With the sizable online community that she has, she could easily fill her retreats with a hundred women, yet she chooses to hold retreats for much smaller groups. I resonated deeply with this choice because I made the same conscious decision to favor greater safety and intimacy with my own retreat offerings. Running intimate, small group retreats with 10-15 women is not necessarily the most profitable choice for my business, but it's the most rewarding choice for my heart and soul.

The sisterhood and support that comes through in a space that is intentionally designed and held for a small group is otherworldly. If you've never experienced this, it's hard to explain the unique magic it is. In this case, small is better than big. Staying small generates a certain quality in the group space, which facilitates life-changing transformation. It allows deeply authentic connections to emerge and mature into lasting form. The bonds forged in such an intimate setting are very different from the connections created in a larger group.

I take a similar approach in my coaching practice. I have committed to take no more than five coaching clients at one time. That commitment aligns with my values, and it also supports me to create the most value. In focused devotion to my clients, I want to make sure that I can be fully present with them. Instead of packing my calendar with appointments, I protect free time and free space for my subconscious to chew on the issues that my clients are facing, even when we're not sitting together on a coaching call. This intentional spaciousness means that I serve fewer clients. But for the few clients that I have, I can show up more fully and I can serve them better.

When slow is better than fast

The growth of my biodegradable glitter business has been erratic. At the beginning, I was selling hand-labeled containers of sparkles out of my backpack. I was sharing and educating people more than I was actually making sales. I was repeatedly having the same uncomfortable conversation, "Do you know what conventional glitter is made of?" I got a lot of puzzled smiles and blank stares. Many people complained that it was too expensive. Others didn't really understand the point. Very few people actually bought biodegradable glitter. Eventually, I launched my online store. For the first year, I offered only four colors for sale. Growth has been slow at times and explosive at times, but growth has never been the primary goal.

My original intent was to provide an eco-friendly alternative to polyester-based glitter for me and my glitter-loving friends. I had no ambitions to build a biodegradable glitter empire. My business growth was organic, entirely fueled by outside forces. My efforts were supported by the viral spread of awareness around ocean plastic pollution, increasing bans on single-use plastic, and the popularity of festivals and other transformational gatherings. It was tempting to ride these trends to greatness. I was encouraged along the way to build an eco-brand empire, trademark the name internationally, and hustle for global distribution. I never did any of those things because they were not aligned with my purpose. My desire was and continues to be: raising ecological awareness, spreading fun and sparkly joy, and working with ease and freedom — all while consciously building a business that reflects my values.

I say no to bulk orders because fulfilling them does not tickle my creative fancy. I say no to developing dozens of new products because it would stress out my mom, who manages production. I say no to collaborations with influencers because I refuse to pay for media play. I say no to selling on Amazon because I want to support small local businesses instead. Have I left money on the table? Have I missed opportunities? Yes. And I celebrate the alignment that comes from those missed opportunities. Saying no to the success myth of bigger and faster frees me to work less, with less stress. It allows me to develop real, human relationships with business partners. It gives me time to research eco-friendly packing materials. It allows me to invest in more costly compostable sugarcane labels, instead of trying to squeeze the largest margin from every sale. It enables me to use the business as a vehicle for my values. My small business is a catalyst for change within the economic ecosystem that I have created, as I encourage retailers, suppliers, and partners to co-evolve with us.

When death becomes the mission

When purpose is manifested into form, we can be sure that that form will die someday. In fact, this death is exactly what purpose is working for, or working towards. The dissolution of the forms we create from purpose is desirable — and actually, inevitable — if we are successful in our purpose work.

Let's consider what happens when we are able to effectively serve, solve, help, or heal whatever it is that we are called to give our gifts to. When we see the desired shift happen — the shift that we have been working for — what do we do then? What we are giving will no longer be needed when the evolutionary arc of humanity transitions into the next phase. When that moment comes, our creation and our contribution is no longer serving higher purpose. If we are lucky enough to witness this shift during our lifetime, then we celebrate! And afterwards, our purpose form must be released so purpose can be rebirthed.

G.K. Chesterton addressed this paradox in defining courage: "Courage is a strong desire to live taking the form of a readiness to die." The same thing can be said about purpose. The embodiment of regenerative purpose is about engaging life fully, while surrendering to death completely. If we live full lives — rich with meaning — then we are loving life completely. So much so, that when we do have to go, the ones we leave behind may grieve us, but they will never miss us. When we move on, the hearts that we have touched are filled to overflowing. And in this way, the love we give keeps moving.

What does this look like in practice? It means taking on the mission of creating a world where your work is ultimately unnecessary. It means growing your impact with the conscious intention to bring about your irrelevance. It means deliberately making moves to hasten your demise instead of trying to fortify your survival. This is tricky business. Below is a Black Friday message that I sent to my eco-glitter customers, which illustrates how I have personally struggled with this dilemma.

> *We are an online company that sells physical products... biodegradable glitter products. So, it's with conflicted feelings that we witness the consumption addiction circus that Black Friday has devolved into over the past several years.*
>
> *It's a moral dilemma that surrounds our very existence. And these are issues we wrestle with daily. Yet we continue to be focused on our "why" — our reason for existing — which is to spread joy and raise consciousness, to champion progress over perfection, and to use our business as a vehicle*

to change the way business is done.

If you want to give physical gifts this holiday season, we encourage you to first consider making gifts yourself or buying them secondhand. And then, and only then, if you're buying new items, please look for products that are sustainably and ethically sourced, and can be cycled back into nature with minimum effort... products that are biodegradable, compostable, reusable, or recyclable. Shop local and shop small, to support families and communities instead of large corporations.

We strive to uphold these ideals in our own sourcing, packaging, partnership, and distribution decisions. If we are ultimately successful in creating the world that we want to see, we know the long game is that there will be no need for companies like ours because the way that we do business will become the norm for all businesses.

While it may seem confusing or contradictory, we deeply appreciate you for supporting our mission and spreading our message by buying our products — and at the same time, we encourage you to buy less and create more in general.

What I am saying here is that I hope I live to see the day this business dies. It's counter-purpose if my attachment to this business prevents its death, when the death of this business could mean that higher purpose is better served. Regenerative purpose puts profit, and even our mere existence, into the service of purpose. Not the other way around.

We miss the true essence of purpose if we treat it as merely personal philosophy or business strategy. Regenerative purpose has a unique frequency that is infused in all aspects of our being and doing. It grounds our presence in every moment. It guides every choice we make and every decision we take. When we surrender the mantle of personal empire building and show up instead for planetary movement making, these purpose-full moves become choiceless choices.

With regenerative purpose, we step into a dance of interdependence where the individual and the collective shape each other as we work. We respond to the world while we receive from it. We reshape the world while we listen to it. The more clearly we see ourselves, the more clearly we can sense the world. The more fully we love ourselves, the more freely we can serve others. The more we can let creation be expressed through us, the more abundance naturally flows through us. We are alive in a dynamic, co-creative, co-evolutionary conversation with reality. We know that gratitude and generosity are side effects of our pure connection to life. Healing ourselves and helping others come together in a Mobius strip of meaning — they may appear to be opposite back-facing sides, but in truth, they merge into a single infinite path of purpose.

CHAPTER 8

The Privilege Effect on Purpose

You do not belong to you. You belong to the universe.
Your significance will remain obscure to you,
but you may assume you are fulfilling your role
if you apply yourself to converting all of your
experiences to the highest advantage of others.
— **Richard Buckminster Fuller**

To have a real conversation about purpose, I think it's important to address the issue of privilege. Examining the intersection of purpose and privilege is a delicate business — an endeavor that is likely to stir up strong emotions, possibly triggering resistance, attracting criticism, or inciting division. Still, I would be remiss to avoid this topic.

I am writing this book from the vantage point (and advantage point) of having a good amount of privilege. I slept in a warm, safe, comfortable bed last night. I had a hearty, nutritious breakfast this morning. I just finished meeting with my writing coach. I now sit at a desk in a coworking space with access to high-speed Internet and an ocean view. I am a homeowner with a condo in San Francisco. I have savings in my bank account. I hold degrees from prestigious educational institutions. I benefit from connections with a network of peers, friends, and colleagues who are similarly well-off.

Your situation may be similar to mine. Or maybe not so much. Even if there are similarities, the details will be different. Though, I will go out on a limb to assert this: If you have the disposable income to acquire this book and the leisure time to take in these words, then you also enjoy some privilege.

The interaction between purpose and privilege is complex, nuanced, and multi-layered. In this chapter, I will outline two basic beliefs around purpose and discuss the implications of those beliefs. The most fundamental difference in these beliefs centers on the question of who purpose is for. Is purpose only a concern for a certain people? Or is purpose something that touches all of humanity? If we choose to believe that purpose is only for the privileged, that belief leads us towards a denial perspective or a savior perspective. If we choose to believe that purpose is for everyone, that belief leads us to appreciation for the broad diversity of purpose expressions, and to honoring the collective rising, knowing that we are all interconnected and interdependent in purpose.

Denial perspective	Purpose is for the privileged. Not everyone has equal access to purpose, so I deny myself the privilege of purpose.
Savior perspective	Purpose is for the privileged. I have more privilege, so I take on purpose work as my duty to those with less privilege.
Diversity perspective	Purpose is a human experience. We embody and express purpose differently according to how much privilege we have.
Collective perspective	Purpose is a human experience. We can make it easier for everyone to embody and express purpose more.

Denial perspective

> Purpose is for the privileged. Not everyone has equal access
> to purpose, so I deny myself the privilege of purpose

Purpose denial is a deflection response that shames the purpose-seeker for being privileged. It dismisses purpose as a "first-world problem" manufactured by whiny elites. "How self-indulgent and silly: the most affluent members of society moaning about feeling unfulfilled! This is narcissistic navel-gazing. How can you be worried about purpose when millions of people can barely feed their families? Stop overanalyzing. Be grateful. You are lucky to have a stable job and a nice home. You must be bored because your life is too easy. Take a seat and give thanks for your healthy paycheck."

If we defer to such privilege shame, then we shush the inner voice that is nudging us to align with more meaningful work. We shrug off purpose as an ideal that is elitist to entertain. We judge ourselves and others as entitled if we choose to own purpose as a desire. This is an excuse to not engage. In order to back up our decision to back off from purpose, we point out that purpose is a problem that only privileged people have.

When we are not ready or willing to engage with what purpose will ask of us, this attitude is a clever strategy to undermine purpose as a valid inquiry. I used this as an excuse myself for years. I managed to ignore the nagging inner voice asking "what else is there to life?" because my life looked good on the outside. I told myself to focus on my blessings and be grateful. This purpose denial helped me protect my self-image; it helped coddle my fear of the unknown; and it helped rationalize my resistance to change. Indulging the barriers created by purpose shame allowed me to procrastinate on exploring my purpose path. I reinforced the "first-world problem" feelings of guilt in order to dismiss the deep inner work that purpose demands.

It is easy to ignore purpose, and color inside the lines. We simply collect paychecks, acquire things, accumulate wealth, and entertain ourselves day in and day out. I did this — and did it well — for nearly 15 years. For a good chunk of that time, I was unaware that anything more was possible for my life. Gradually, I came to know better. I knew that I was not contributing my most precious gifts to the world. I knew that I was not creating the life I most desired. I started to see how I was complicit with my complacency. By not changing, I was passively perpetuating patriarchal power structures that I would rather see die. Eventually I could no longer pretend not to know these things.

Savior perspective

> Purpose is for the privileged. I have more privilege, so I take on purpose work as my duty to those with less privilege

With this next approach, we still hold the baseline belief that purpose is reserved for a chosen few. The purpose savior is someone who reaches out to help from a place of superiority. We believe that purpose is limited edition. Purpose is the purview of those born in a safe, stable economy. It is only possible for those living in peace, under relatively functional governments. It is only viable for those who receive adequate healthcare and nutrition to grow up strong and vital, without debilitating diseases. It is only achievable for those who have education and opportunities. Here we are no longer denying purpose as a valid line of inquiry, rather we feel privileged enough to take on purpose as our solemn duty.

When we view purpose as a moral imperative, we can become more connected to the field of support around us. We are grateful for the options that privilege provides and we are motivated to use those options to benefit others. We realize that those struggling to meet basic safety and survival needs may not have as much space to explore or express purpose. Within this inequity we find a reason to engage. Seeing that not everyone can easily access purpose, we feel a sense of duty to those less fortunate to get on with our purpose work.

This is a noble take on purpose. If we believe that only a select subset of humans can engage in meaningful work, and we see ourselves as one of the lucky ones, it can give us a strong drive for service. We accept our privilege and we accept that what comes with it, is a duty to help others. The trouble with this is that it can feel heavy to be in this role, where we feel the weight of the world on our shoulders. When service is taken on as a burden, it suffocates creativity and restricts Receptivity.

We need to mind the risks of the savior complex. Feeling obliged to serve others, it is easy to neglect our own needs. Driven by our good intentions, we can also cause unintended harm. The oxygen mask rule applies here. Airplane safety demonstrations remind us to put on our own oxygen mask before helping others. We cannot serve others without saving ourselves. We cannot help others without healing ourselves. In fact, if we martyr ourselves to service, we will be blocked from bringing forth our highest and best gifts to the world.

If we set out as a self-appointed savior, we won't get very far. The savior role quickly gets heavy. It is not our job to single-handedly save the planet. It is not our responsibility to be a hero or heroine for humanity. I had to remind myself of this truth often while writing this book, in order to keep going. If I let my ego get caught up in thoughts about how my work will help others, the whole process would quickly start to feel sludgy. I would start to worry whether I am good enough. I would start to wonder whether I am doing the right things.

Again, and again, I keep coming back to how my purpose work is healing me. I have to tell myself that even if no one reads or benefits from this book, the year that I spent birthing it is still worthwhile because of all the lessons the book has given me throughout the creation process. It might turn out that what I have done to bring this book into the world is also an act of service to you, dear reader, but before it can be that, it must first be a profound act of self-love for me.

Diversity perspective

Purpose is a human experience.
We embody and express purpose differently according to
how much privilege we have

If we say that purpose is only for the privileged, then we must draw an arbitrary line of separation between "purpose haves" and "purpose have-nots." On one side of the line, there are people for whom purpose is possible and on the other side there are other people for whom it is out of reach. The question is, where do we draw that line? Who decides where the line is?

Let's see what happens if we democratize access to purpose instead. What if we assume that purpose is possible for every person on the planet? We might experience some cognitive dissonance with this when we look around because we see many people who appear to be unfulfilled or frustrated, or who are struggling just to survive in day-to-day life. The thing is, we have no idea whether other people experience a sense of purpose in their lives or not. Purpose is an inside job. Purpose is not something that we can see in another as an outside observer. Maybe all those seemingly purposeless people don't actually need to change anything to do better at purpose. Maybe it is our way of looking at purpose that needs adjustment instead.

Going back to one of the reframes for the new purpose paradigm: Purpose is not a form; it is a frequency. Here we need to look at the conditioned beliefs we have around what a purpose-full life looks like and feels like. We might have this idea that our purpose work needs to be substantive and scalable. That is not true. Purpose can be the lasting legacy of a lifetime of work and it can also be expressed in a momentary interaction. It can touch millions of people and it can also touch just one person. Purpose does not prescribe any particular size or shape.

The idea that those with less privilege cannot have purpose is disempowering as well as demeaning. Purpose exists because we exist. It is our nature. It is an experience that is possible for all humans. The purpose served by those with less privilege is just commonly unseen or devalued by others. Ironically, it is usually least recognized by those with lots of privilege.

Take for example, the single dad who works nights so he can send his two daughters to school. His purpose might be to provide a stable home and a positive male role model for them. He may not articulate or even recognize this as his purpose. Yet this is the foundation for every choice he makes, every day. Think of the barista who pours perfect lattes for anxiety-ridden commuters every morning. Her purpose might be to inject some warmth or wisdom into an otherwise banal day for her patrons. This kind of purpose may not be packaged into a punchy personal mission statement. Yet this purpose pervades every smile, every kind word, and every interaction.

To have purpose is to be human. Purpose is not reserved for an elite few. We simply need to adjust the lens through which we perceive purpose to include a wider range of expressions.

Collective perspective

Purpose is a human experience. We can make it easier for everyone to embody and express purpose more

If we believe that purpose exists within each and every one of us, then how do we reconcile the fact that purpose is embodied to different degrees and expressed in different forms?

No matter how much privilege we have, we all experience some obstacles to purpose alignment. These obstacles might be structural, systemic, circumstantial, or psychological barriers. The way these challenges impact us will vary based on our privilege. Some obstacles to purpose are disproportionately faced by those with less privilege. Health issues. Resource constraints. Systemic biases. There are real and present survival demands that we face in physical reality. Having dependents or student debt can burden us on our purpose path. If we are struggling to cover childcare, mortgage payments, car repairs, and credit card bills, then purpose is most likely not at the top of our priority list. The concept of purpose may not even register in our awareness in a way that is namable and noticeable.

Each of us lives somewhere along a privilege spectrum. What privilege does, is it expands the set of options for purpose expression. When we have more privilege, we have a larger set of possible purpose forms to choose from. Highly privileged people have more choices to make. This expanded possibility adds complexity. Having more choices also means having more potential distractions and diversions. The more privilege we have, the more ways we can get off track. Having less privilege means having a smaller set of options. There are still choices to make, but there's not as much range of movement. Every decision carries greater relative risk. Yet having fewer choices means there are also fewer ways to get lost.

With more privilege, we have access to more resources, support, and opportunities. With more privilege, our purpose form has the potential to impact more people. In other words, when we have more privilege, our purpose form has greater power and broader influence. The power of being high-privilege can be abdicated and it can also be abused. We have to be a bit careful when we have a lot of privilege. It means navigating outside influences that are attracted by this power, which may try to hijack our high-privilege vehicle to serve ends other than higher purpose.

In addition to having to navigate more potential distractions and diversions, high privilege also makes it easy to judge others as "not doing the right things" because *they* are not behaving in alignment with *our* values. It's important to remember that our perceptions are colored by our own set of options. Being able to make values-based decisions is indeed a privilege, one that some may not be able to afford. This is why it's so important to do our own work, and stay in our own swim lane. Instead of judging others for falling short, we can help elevate others' purpose expression by working to dismantle unjust systems.

Regardless of how much privilege we enjoy, we can all expand in our experience of purpose. The expansion could be external and visible in what we create, share, promote, and support. The expansion could also be wholly internal. It could be a subtle inner shift that allows us to infuse whatever we are already doing with a deeper quality of love. Ultimately, purpose comes alive and becomes aligned in us when love is omnipresent in how we relate with the world.

Because we are interconnected, the expansion of purpose in one's individual reality will ripple through the expansion of purpose in our shared reality. As we personally live and work on purpose more, so do others, and so do we all. The "me" and "we" merge, as the realization of place and meaning reverberates through the network effect of regenerative purpose.

Purpose is not exclusively reserved for those with high

privilege. Rather it is an experience reserved for the bold-hearted, steel-willed, and thick-skinned. Purpose does not come through those content with being comfortable. It takes courage to step out of the system of extraction and exploitation. It takes strength to escape the trap of consumption and competition. It takes conviction to choose the uncertainty of purpose over the security of the program. But we can do it.

CHAPTER 9

Self-Transcendence and Survival

*The more man forgets himself by giving himself to a cause
to serve or another person to love,
the more human he becomes and the more he actualizes
himself. Self-actualization is possible only as a
side-effect of self-transcendence.*
— **Viktor Frankl**

Purpose. Meaning. Fulfillment. With these clumsy words, we attempt to triangulate the enigmatic essence of human existence. Perhaps at best, we can only paint an incomplete picture, trying to describe the art of living a well-lived life. The words that we have to express and explain this are frustratingly limiting, but I think ultimately what we are trying to point to is the messy beauty of being fully human and fully here.

We are currently living through a pivotal moment in human history. We have reached an unprecedented level of health and prosperity globally, and we enjoy a lot of convenience and efficiency thanks to incredible advances in technology. At the same time, we are also facing anxiety-inducing uncertainty. Human separation and suffering are now teeming and the global climate and ecological emergency is painfully acute.

Intuitively, we sense that purpose is medicine for many of the illnesses we are afflicted with in this time. Purpose can help us reconnect our relationship with the family of humanity. Purpose can help us find harmony with nature. Purpose can help us remember abundance, reclaim wholeness, and restore health to the planet. To evoke the healing benefits of genuine, soul-sourced purpose, we need to take care with the way we wield it. Purpose is misused if individuals lay claim to it as a label, in order to present themselves as more evolved or accomplished. Likewise, purpose is abused if organizations use it as a carrot or a stick, in order to move or manipulate people.

We need to reframe the way we think about purpose, and we need to reform the way we work with purpose. The kind of purpose we need now is not a single focus; not a definitive concept; not a personal mission; not a final destination; not a particular form. No, it is none of those things. Regenerative purpose is the dynamic experience and dedicated practice of living in co-creative conversation with the wholeness of life.

Regenerative purpose is the current of life that flows through us when we are authentic, attuned, responsive, and receptive. This energetic charge that we experience from this is life force moving. We feel enlivened in presence and aligned in movement when we are in this purpose flow. We know that we are all one, but we are not all the same. Think of the human body, which is made up of trillions of cells, with each cell fulfilling a unique role in the health and function of the whole person. In the same way, the living body of humanity is made up of billions of individuals. The health of the global organism that we are part of depends on our ability to communicate and connect with each other in service to the whole.

When we take on regenerative purpose work, the act of saving ourselves and the act of serving others are no longer in opposition — these two efforts merge into the same endeavor. This is not for the faint-hearted. Engaging in this work will challenge you to the core. It will bring you to your personal evolutionary edge again and again. If you believe you are doing your purpose work now and you have reached a place where it feels quite comfortable, then watch out. Another opportunity to up-level may be coming soon. There may be a new calling that will ask you to step in or step up. Our purpose work is always guiding us gently to grow and expand. It teaches us to be still with more lightness, and to move intentionally with more freedom. As we become more available for purpose, we learn to surf our personal evolutionary edge while serving the evolution of collective consciousness.

Self-actualization and self-transcendence

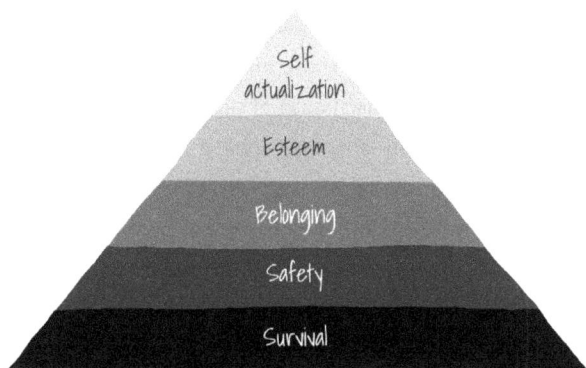

Self
actualization

Esteem

Belonging

Safety

Survival

For Abraham Maslow, life purpose was connected with self-actualization — the realization and expression of individual potential. According to his classic pyramid depicting the human hierarchy of needs, there is a sequence or stacking of needs fulfillment. In this, self-actualization marks the highest level of human development. At the top of the pyramid, the individual realizes full person-hood; it is at this stage or level where the individual's potential becomes actual.

According to Maslow, there is a priority order for getting our needs met, and these needs can be organized into five stages or levels. When our lower level needs are taken care of, we see more space opening up for our higher level needs to be addressed. The hierarchy of a pyramidal structure may seem to imply that we have a linear sequence of needs being met one after the other, with one quest being completed before the next one is initiated. However, on a practical level, I believe that all of these needs cohabit our psychological space, and we are looking for ways to meet all of them all of the time. If we see Maslow's categories of needs as both layered and leveled as well as interrelated and overlapping, we might see how when one level of need is mostly or fully met, then the next level need becomes more central as our primary motivator. To relate these phases of needs fulfillment to our discussion of privilege, we might say that we have more and more space to engage in purpose expression with increasing amounts of privilege. As we reach more advanced stages of needs fulfillment, we have more capacity available to address our self-actualization needs; we can afford to invest more attention and energy into the exploration of purpose work. The more resourced we are, the longer we can afford to stand in the gap between the old paradigm and the new paradigm as the rest of humanity joins us.

What is fascinating to me is that Dr. Maslow was plagued

by two questions in the later part of his life. He wondered: (1) What motivates people who have already self-actualized? (2) Why do some self-actualized people still behave badly? Eventually, he addressed these concerns by adding another further need beyond self-actualization at the top of the pyramid, which he labeled as self-transcendence.

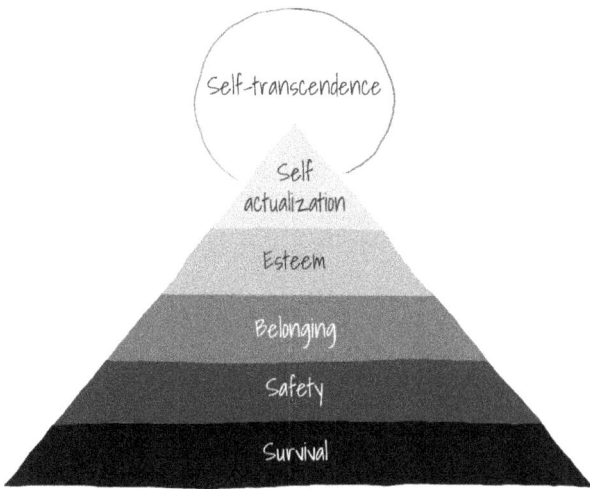

Maslow described self-transcendence as a state of higher consciousness marked by feelings of awe, ecstasy, connection, and sacredness. Self-transcendence can also be defined as the expansion of awareness beyond the body-based boundaries of our egoic self. It is the shift in consciousness that takes place when we move away from identifying with the personal and move towards recognizing our self-hood as one of many expressions of the transpersonal.

Self-transcendence is the realm of no-self. This is where our individual identity dissolves. Lines of separation bend, blur, and disappear as we surrender to interconnectedness with all of life. We relax our empire-building agendas and we become water molecules in a wave. As Paul Wong writes, "The self does not exist as an island. It is embedded in a vast web of relationships. Metaphorically, we are but one drop of water in an ocean of relationships. We will naturally pursue and practice self-transcendence when we realize that we are all related both horizontally and vertically — we are connected with a higher power and with other people."

At the level of self-transcendence, Maslow believed that people who had already met their own personal needs for self-actualization would mainly be motivated by a desire to help others to self-actualize. Maslow's idea is consistent with how we might see purpose taking shape for high-privilege people. As we discussed in the previous chapter, those with more privilege essentially have more power and they can use this power to help those with less privilege to embody and express more purpose.

We come full spiral

In the new paradigm of purpose, the personal and transpersonal dimensions are both present. The individual is engaged in co-creative conversation with the collective. Purpose flow is a natural process that is both impermanent and interdependent. It is not purely self and it is not purely no-self — the engagement of both self and no-self are critical to the dynamic alignment of regenerative purpose.

With the words of Viktor Frankl cited at the start of this chapter, we are reminded of how important it is to give ourselves in loving service; this is what brings us home to our own humanness and helps us actualize our potential. Frankl alludes to the co-creative dance of the individual and the collective as he marries the concepts of self-actualization and self-transcendence. In his view, these two things are intertwined as one gives rise to the other.

The pyramid is not the best shape to represent this kind of interdependent dynamic. The pyramid is good for illustrating a fixed hierarchy, chronological sequence, or linear progression — none of which reflect the new paradigm of purpose. The circle, on the other hand, more appropriately suggests the fluid, cyclical, simultaneous, and symbiotic movement of regenerative purpose. Humanity is part of nature and the purpose of human life is the art of nature. As participants in the raw chaos of human existence, we know that it is not as neat or as logical as a pyramid would suggest. We know the destination is an illusion; the process is never-ending; and we only arrive at an end in order to start again.

The poetry of the present moment is that we can see self-transcendence and survival (the top and the bottom levels of Maslow's modified pyramid) now converging. In the pursuit of individual safety, comfort, and other egoic concerns, we have grown inflated with hubris, isolated from each other, and disconnected from nature. Forgetting our place as part of nature has led us to the verge of self-induced extinction. Now self-transcendence is no longer just a nice philosophy. It has immediate, personal, and practical implications for us today. Self-transcendence is now a matter of survival. We need to get over ourselves in order to save ourselves.

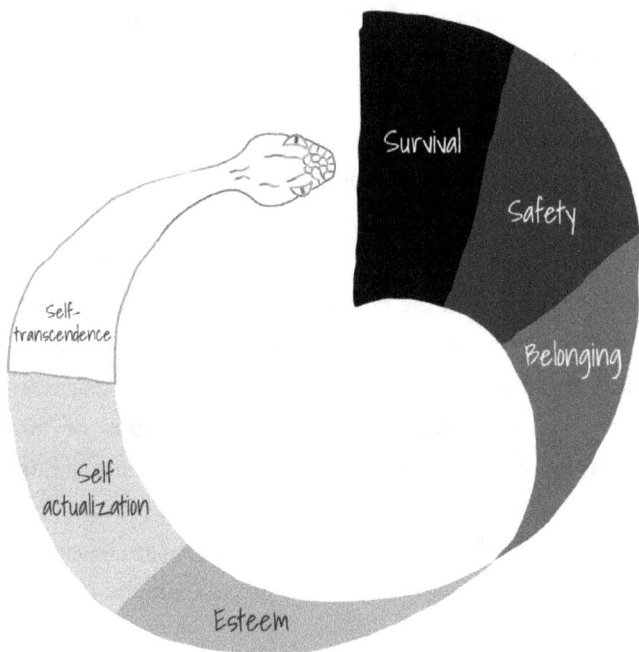

Let's imagine turning the pyramid on its side, stretching it out like a noodle, and transforming it into a spiral of expansion. With self-transcendence turning back around to approach survival, we see the image of the *ouroboros* emerging — a snake eating its own tail. We have now come full circle to form a spiral. Self-transcendence becomes both necessary and urgent, as we move from the survival of a single human to the collective survival of humanity. The lofty spiritual aspirations of ego-transcendence may seem light-years away from the basic, biological, survival needs of our animal body. But right now, moving beyond the body while still inhabiting a body is essential for the continuation of the human race. We need to relax our personal concerns in order to fully participate in the collective waves of change. When we can manage this transition, humanity will enter the next cycle of expansion.

The end is the beginning

It feels slightly odd and strangely perfect for me to conclude this book with someone else's words. But then, part of me likes it because it reinforces the fact that this book is a community creation. This is not *my* book, this is *our* book.

My work has been to perceive and receive, to tune into what was personally activating for me, and to move from love in creating this book, while staying true to my authentic self. I embraced the book-birthing process as my purpose work. This book has transformed me at the same time it was being created through me. I am a messenger but I do not own the message. I have written a book but I do not claim the identity of "writer." With the publication of this book, my hope is to free myself from the self-concepts that have grown up around me and inside me during this creation journey, so that I can be fully available for life's next calling, whatever it is.

I have been supported and guided in countless ways in the process of bringing this book into being. You will soon see in the acknowledgements section the vastness of the virtual village that has come together around the creation of this book. But first, let's wrap this up.

I concluded my purpose interviews by asking people to share a few nuggets of wisdom or personal advice for the readers of this book — readers who I imagined might be longing for a sense of purpose, or curious to know how purpose could impact their lives. When I listened to Daan Gorter answer this question, my body was in shivers and tears came to my eyes. I knew then that

I wanted his words to become the closing for this book. And now, they are that. I leave his words here as an invitation and an invocation for you, dear reader.

Go forth and purpose.

If you feel lost at this moment in your life, or you don't have any idea what purpose means, or you don't feel that you have found "your purpose" yet... Don't worry about it. It's very normal to be here right now. Many of us have been here. It's a good place to be, because it's inviting you to self-inquiry. It's inviting you to step out of all the conditioning and programming that you have accumulated over the course of your life.

Know that all your life experiences are bringing you to where you are right now and they are motivating you to explore different paths. But also know that these experiences do not define who you are. And they definitely do not define what you are here to do.

You have the full potential to explore an infinite number of paths, without any kind of limitations. This exploration is a joyful, creative, inspiring process. It is a process full of fun and also full of setbacks. It's a journey of ups and downs. But when you really choose; when you make a decision; when you commit yourself to this journey, the treasures that lie in front of you are beyond what you can imagine. I truly wish for you to find the same sense of meaning, and excitement, and beauty that I experience today in my life.

I embarked on my purpose journey eight years ago and I surrounded myself with people who had the same question.

We traveled together. I now see that all of us — those who deeply committed themselves to this process — are now living in realities that would have been beyond our wildest dreams when we started.

You should also know that it is a nonstop inquiry process. From time to time, I still ask myself the same questions today as I asked myself eight years ago. The only thing is, the clarity of the answers is increasing. The response I get from the universe is that what I am doing is exactly what I need to be doing in every moment. It is just magical.

Purpose Practices

*Instead of thinking about solving your whole life, just
think about adding additional good things, one at a time.
Just let your pile of good things grow.*
— Rainbow Rowell

When we start to notice experiences that connect us with purpose, we start to experience them more frequently. We keep adding to our pile of good things and watching it grow. This takes place organically and effortlessly, in my experience. Purpose is not a problem that we need to solve. There is no stress or strife required to let purpose flow.

Of course, we can also develop our qualities of Authenticity, Attunement, Responsiveness, and Receptivity and thereby create more space for purpose flow to move through us. There is a myriad of approaches available to help us intentionally cultivate these four core qualities. This section contains a catalog of tools and practices that are suggested for personal exploration. They are offered as inspiration for where you might start looking. They are not intended as instructions for what you should be doing.

Purpose practices for cultivating Authenticity

Self-inquiry with typology systems

Authenticity is supported by connecting with the truth of who we are and how we are in each moment — with everything included. To access our Genius in Fluid Truth, we must first break through the layers of performance and programming that hide the truth. One of the main ways that we block Authenticity is by repeatedly acting out the same personality patterns over and over and mistaking them for who we truly are. We need to get to know our core patterns and befriend them so that we can move through and beyond them.

My friend Ezra Sandzer-Bell shared the parable of an alligator with me:

Our personality patterns are like alligators that we feed with our attention and energy. We have fed these alligators our entire lives so we don't think much about it; we do it automatically. Every so often, the alligator bites our hand.

Not hard enough to take off a finger, but certainly hard enough that it hurts. When it happens, we chide the alligator, "Ouch! Hey, why did you do that? That wasn't nice." And if alligators could shrug, it would probably shrug and say, "What did you expect? This is what alligators do."

This parable illustrates the challenge of disengaging egoic patterns. These patterns can be so tangled in our identity that we do not see any other option than to feed them. If the alligator represents a pattern that we have fed for a long time, it is pointless to hope we can change the alligator's behavior because it is his inalienable nature to bite us. What is powerful is choosing to change how we interact with the alligator. We don't waste our energy wishing for the alligator to show up differently. We meet the alligator differently instead. We stop feeding it and feigning surprise when we get bitten. This is how we learn to coexist peacefully with our patterns — seeing and accepting their nature without continuing to enable and energize them.

There are many typology systems that categorize human beings, whether based on behaviors, motivations, preferences, or dharma. These systems allow us to get intimate with our alligators. The Enneagram is one such system that describes nine archetypal ego patterns — nine species of alligator — each with a core desire and core fear fueling its activity. It shows us predictable, patterned ways that we protect, defend, or promote our sense of self. It provides a roadmap to recognize, accept, and try to balance the patterns we have become overly identified with.

Seeing through our ego patterns happens retrospectively at first. When we take on the project of self-examination, we usually start by looking back at everything that has happened up until now. As we get better acquainted with our patterns, we begin to notice them in the moment as they are happening. Eventually, we start to see our patterns *before* they play out. And from there, we have a choice — to feed the alligator, or to not feed the alligator. Do we engage in the pattern the same way that we always have, or do we choose something new and different?

Self-assessments can be powerful tools, yet any system that sorts humans into various types should be used with caution. Even Carl Jung, whose theories form the foundation for the popular Myers-Briggs Type Indicator (MBTI) assessment, has said, "It is not the purpose of psychological typology to classify human beings into categories — this in itself would be pretty pointless." There are three things to be wary of when using personality tests.

- Self-report personal assessments only work to the extent that we are aware and honest with ourselves. If you are disconnected from your experiences or uncertain about your motivations, you will miss a lot. On the flip side, if you are overly confident that you already know everything there is to know about yourself, you can also manipulate the results of an assessment to confirm the familiar lies that you tell yourself.

- Don't let any diagnostic results lull you into the comfort of complacency. The value in examining our patterns lies in the process of self-inquiry not in the supposed answer. If you do use a self-assessment to facilitate exploration of your patterns, remember that your assessment result is the beginning of the discovery process, not the end.

- Be careful about affixing assessment results to an identity badge. Statements such as "I am an introvert" or "I am a helper" may seem innocuous, but there is a trap in such declarations. If we get locked into identification with these self-concepts, they will constrict the Authenticity that is needed to unlock Genius in Fluid Truth. We need to view self-assessment test results as being merely a snapshot in time; they can only capture a limited impression of a constantly-evolving narrative.

How does understanding typology help us cultivate more Authenticity? Seeing through the ego patterns that we have confused with who we are helps us decouple our habits from our choices. Once we recognize our most persistent patterns of thought and emotion, we can loosen the grip they have on the way we live. Instead of identifying with our patterns and reinforcing them, we can learn new and different ways to interact with our alligators. My teacher Russ Hudson always emphasizes, "The Enneagram is not about showing you the box you're in so you can live and die inside that box. It's about showing you the box you're in so you can find the keys to get out of it." The same can be said for any system used to sort humans.

Shadow integration

Authenticity calls for us to embrace forbidden or forgotten parts of ourselves — known as our shadow — so that a fuller version of our true self is available to engage.

Growing up, we observe others' reactions to our behavior. We learn from this feedback what is desired or expected from us and what is not. We conform to these influences. As children, our very survival depends on this adaptation. We reveal some parts of ourselves and hide others. We get used to showing up as a carefully curated, edited, and framed persona. We leave out everything else and stash it in a corner. Stepping into Authenticity, we can reclaim those dusty treasures. We stop disowning the parts that conflict with our self-concept. We stop denying the parts that seem inconvenient. We stop deleting the parts that catch us by surprise.

Somatic trauma therapist James Hady shared a brilliant example of how getting stuck in a self-concept of, "I am the authentic one," can actually become inauthentic.

> *I was in a phase where I was breaking out of my MBA fakeness and stepping into authenticity and vulnerability. I began to share publicly about things that were pretty hard for me to discuss at that time — deep emotions, personal traumas, and inner struggles. I received a lot of positive feedback on my Facebook posts. Friends told me that they were moved — sometimes to tears. It felt incredible and freeing to own and share these shadows and receive all this attention, affirmation, and loving acceptance.*

> *For a while it became my "thing" to be this authentic masculine voice that was exposing individual and collective shadows, but slowly and surprisingly this became a trap too. Soon sharing deep dark emotional "shadows" became the norm for my self-expression. Then anything that wasn't deep dark and emotional became my shadow! I felt limited in expressing my judgments and raw desires. I struggled to share*

laughter and playfulness. It was hard to even let myself take a break from all the feels and just not give a fuck for once. As one teacher pointed out, I was now performing authenticity.

What would have been truly authentic (and utterly terrifying for me) then was to let myself be a regular human, fully owning my horniness, pride, biases, entitlement, and enjoyment of superficial pleasures. Being normal was the new shadow!

In some schools of thought, shadow work focuses solely on bringing to light the dark, negative aspects of our nature that lurk outside of our conscious awareness. More broadly speaking, shadow work includes the revelation of anything that is hidden. The shadow is not necessarily dark. It can include unknown positive aspects or secret strengths as well. The hidden treasures that we forget or disown are sometimes called the golden shadow. In James's case, what had fallen into shadow was any part of his experience that he considered to be lighthearted, playful, pleasurable, or even mundane. As we were exploring this topic, James noted that, "It's not just that you 'should' be authentic. Being authentic and embracing your shadow side actually floods you with energy and feelings of aliveness, and often clarifies direction."

The tricky thing about shadow work is that, by definition, our shadow is something that we cannot see. We don't know what we don't know. Nobel laureate Thomas Schelling once keenly observed, "One thing a person cannot do, no matter how rigorous his analysis or how heroic his imagination, is to draw up a list of things that would never occur to him."

However, what we can see clearly are the shadows that we

project onto others. James shared this as one of the most effective techniques for shadow integration:

> *Think about the people that trigger us the most. What are the things they do, not that just annoy us, but the things that really hit a nerve. Then we look inward and do the really hard self-inquiry in seeing how in actuality, we are the same as them, we've done the same things, we've been the same way. That in and of itself is hard enough already. We can take it a step further to see how those behaviors or mindsets or values can actually be good. This inquiry process challenges our own values. It is like when the Light side sees the Dark side and then realizes, actually, the Dark isn't really Dark and the Light isn't really Light. In that opening, the dichotomy melts and shadows integrate.*

We reveal more latent potential and broaden our range of movement when we integrate our shadow — both positive and negative aspects. By including more of what has historically been pushed outside the edges of our self-concept, we can access more of our true selves.

Mind your inside voice

Whether we are aware or not, we are constantly talking to ourselves and that self-talk is usually dominated by a few recurring narratives. The storylines that are repeating in our heads are critical in shaping our mindscape and subsequently, shifting our reality. They are more than idle chatter; they are powerful tools for change. When we start to look deeper, we might find that our inner dialogue is heavily determined by limiting beliefs — ideas that we have about ourselves or our reality that prevent us from embracing new ways of being.

Before we can mind the language that we use to speak to ourselves, first we have to listen to what is dominating our inner dialogue. With awareness, we can review the programs we are running in the context of connections with others. Our partners, friends, and colleagues can be excellent mirrors for us because they are exposed to the repeated expression of our patterns. However, the dynamics in personal relationships can sometimes prevent clear seeing because the other party is engaged in patterns as well. This is why engaging a professional therapist to serve as a guide for us in a counseling relationship can be supportive.

There are also some powerful methods available for us to work on our internal narratives without professional help. *The Work* by Byron Katie is a self-inquiry tool that we can use to unpack our existing beliefs and thought structures. It is a simple but profound process of examining and reconsidering the beliefs that constrain our reality. We can use Byron Katie's technique to look into our mind's creations by asking ourselves a series of four questions: (1) Is it true? (2) Can you absolutely know that it's true? (3) How do you react and what happens when you believe that thought? (4) Who would you be without that thought?

Once we discover the detrimental self-talk we want to delete, we might also want to install new narratives that are more supportive to our growth. Positive affirmations are a popular way to do this. Affirmations are declarative statements expressing a future desired state in the present tense. These can be effective if used with finesse. If used clumsily, they can lead to bypassing underlying issues, or attacking our beliefs too aggressively — like taking a sledgehammer to a pin nail. If our affirmations are too far afield from our current reality, our mind will reflexively say "that's not true" and create resistance or even outright rejection of the idea.

Conscious-business coach Francesco Marcuccio introduced me to a subtler way to shift our beliefs, which I refer to as graduated affirmations. Affirmations usually entail writing down one statement of a desired future state, which often seems impossible from where we sit right now. With a graduated affirmation, we write down that one "out there" statement and then break it down into component parts or interim steps.

Here is a personal example to illustrate how this works. My core statement of affirmation is:

> *I am loved, safe, seen, supported, desired, and chosen by a mature, self-aware, and honest man; he has enough money, is devoted to purpose work, and is committed to deepening intimacy in a long-term partnership that elevates our individual soul paths.*

That single affirmation can feel like too much to ask for if it seems very foreign to me in my current reality. Standing alone, it can trigger a lot of subconscious "no way" and "yeah right" and "that's impossible" in my mind. What can I do to override that programming? How can I loosen the grip of these limiting beliefs? I can break down the affirmation into bite-size pieces that feel more believable or more possible to my psyche. These sub-level statements represent various dimensions of the core statement or incremental steps towards realizing that reality.

The component statements or steps in my graduated affirmation are:

- I hold and love myself through the full spectrum of life's experiences and emotions.
- I am surrounded and supported by men who recognize and appreciate my qualities.
- I allow myself to receive from men without needing to perform to earn their gifts.
- I open my heart vulnerably and offer unconditional love without expectations.
- I share my truth and honor my boundaries, welcoming rejection as redirection.
- I develop deep friendships with men grounded in shared joy in the present moment.

These statements feel closer to my current reality and I can already see evidence of them in my life right now. The more I can connect with these component statements as reflective of my lived experience, the more I move towards the core statement becoming true. Our long-held limiting beliefs are hidden under many layers of ego protection. We cannot banish them with a few wishful words; they need more subtle coaxing to loosen their grip on our psyche.

The more we can see through the ego patterns that we mistake for who we are, the more we can be present and connected to our true self. The more we can free ourselves from the limiting beliefs that we mistake for facts, the more room there is for Authenticity to flourish.

Purpose practices for cultivating Attunement

Manage your media diet

An extreme solution for this signal overload might be to completely shut down from receiving inputs. Rolf Dobelli argues in *The Guardian* article "Why News is Bad for You" that news is useless because it does nothing to motivate engagement and contribution. On the contrary, he says it victimizes and paralyzes. After four years on a strict, zero news diet, Dobelli reported finding "less disruption, less anxiety, deeper thinking, more time, and more insights."

The idea of shielding ourselves from media influences entirely might sound tempting, but to cultivate Attunement, we have to stay connected. The trick is to stay connected with what is happening in the world without getting overwhelmed. We need to learn to tune ourselves in to receive important signals without being distracted by the noise.

It is important to monitor the amount of time that we spend with media, the types of information and sources that we are accessing, as well as the kinds of activities that we are engaging in. Embodying the quality of Attunement is about paying selective attention. We create that selective attention by curating the information we consume. We must watch what we read as much as we watch what we eat.

Whether it is with information or objects, we want to be mindful of maintaining a healthy balance of consuming versus creating. For most of us, we tend to consume a lot more content than we create. This can be a very challenging habit to break because our information ecosystem is designed to be maximally addictive. Words, colors, icons, devices — everything has been crafted to capture and keep our attention.

There are some habit-busting techniques that we can use to opt out of information addiction. When we are trying to develop healthier eating habits for example, fasting can help reboot our relationship with food. By not eating any food for a while, we deliberately interrupt our addictive loops and introduce a moment of pause to consider what we are doing. Similarly, a media fast can help reset our relationship with information and communication devices. Temporary withdrawal from our usual objects of addiction increases our level of consciousness around what we consume, whether it is food or media.

When we intentionally choose our media diet, it is possible to find a healthier balance between provocation and inspiration. We need to become more aware of what is entering our headspace and how it is getting there. If we see something that does not belong in our newsfeed or our inbox, then let's take a minute to make sure we don't see it again. Delete what is not needed immediately. Use the unfollow option and unsubscribe buttons early and often. Use apps to help monitor the time spent fixated on screens. We have levers at our disposal to help us curate the influences that come before our eyes or into our ears; we often just forget to use them.

Just say no to everything

Saying "yes" to everything — as parodied in the Jim Carrey movie *Yes Man* — helps us engage. It encourages us to try new things. The practice of saying "no" on the other hand, clarifies our values and confronts our fear of disappointing others. When we free-up space from the clutter of external expectations, it can be filled with what truly matters. The practice of saying "no" helps us bust our people-pleasing habits and clear space for Attunement.

Saying "yes" when we mean "no" has a number of undesirable effects.

- *Expectations.* When you automatically say "yes" without considering your own desires and limits, you train people to treat you like a "yes man" or "yes woman." The increasing burden of expectations can lead to being overloaded and overwhelmed.

- *Disempowerment.* Habitually giving in to others' whims and demands while suppressing your own voice robs you of your creative will and individual agency. You become a victim of circumstance instead of owning the creation of your experience.

- *Resentment.* If you nod your head "yes" while secretly shaking "no" on the inside, this generates dissonance or tension, which can deteriorate into resentment.

- *Loss of trust.* If your inner conflict is obvious, it can erode trust. Others might feel they have to guess at what you mean. Never saying "no" suggests a lack of boundaries that saps power from our positive agreements. Your "yes" loses its power.

Of course, saying no to *everything* is an exaggeration. What is most important — and most growth-inducing — is the practice of saying "no" to things that we habitually say "yes" to. This stretch zone looks different for each of us. For me, it might be saying no to spending excessive amounts of time with a friend needing emotional support after a tough breakup. That is my personal kryptonite: a friend in need. The "no"-ing practice can focus on any number of things. It might be saying "no" to casual sex with someone we find attractive, if we have a pattern of saying "yes" there. It might be saying "no" to working on the weekend to meet an unreasonable deadline, if we feel tortured by the idea of displeasing our boss. It might be saying "no" to a party invitation and staying home, if we struggle with a fear of missing out.

Author Elizabeth Gilbert makes a compelling case for saying "no" in order to say yes to purpose:

> *I knew what I wanted to do (write) and I knew how I wanted to do it (with joyful energy) … and so many, many things had to be let go. You would choke on your cornflakes if I told you some of the things I've said no to in my lifetime. Beautiful opportunities. Gorgeous adventures. Fun experiences. The chance to meet amazing people. And so many weekday night invitations, to go out for drinks with friends.*

(Weekends, too, often.) I would have loved to have done all those things. But there is only one of me. And I know what I really want to be doing with my life, and I know what it takes to create that sort of devoted focus.

We overload our calendars as a clever ruse to avoid facing our fears and ignore our nagging inner voice. After leaving my corporate job, I had (and still have a tendency towards) several addictions to distraction. For example, I was often changing locations as a digital nomad. The mental load of managing travel logistics, coupled with a constant state of transition, kept my mind restless. I was also enrolling in endless workshops, retreats, and training programs, which consumed my time and depleted my savings. I had to learn to say "no" to many, many things.

I often work with my coaching clients to define a "not to do" list. This list is designed to exclude addictive yesses. Our addictive behaviors tend to crowd our physical and psychological space, which means there is less space for new insights and opportunities to enter. When the form of our purpose work is nascent or not yet clear, it is delicate and sensitive to negative impact from outside influences. Honoring these exclusions is a way of building a fence around our baby tree to protect it in the early stages of growth. We say "no" to block out the usual activities that we use to stay busy and drop the usual excuses to procrastinate on purpose work.

Whatever the domain in which we are habitually yessing, we can take a time-out. By saying "no" instead of "yes," we break away from the familiar and give surprises a chance to emerge. We don't need to apologize, justify, explain, or defend our decision to decline. Basic self-care is more about boundaries than it is about bubble baths, and having good boundaries helps us create the space that is necessary for the cultivation of Attunement.

Connect to body wisdom

Our body contains a universe of wisdom that many of us rarely access. Western education teaches us to prioritize the rational, logical, and practical machinations of the mind above other centers of intelligence. To access our true inner authority, it is helpful to connect with multiple centers. We can commune with our mind; consider our heart; and consult our body.

Body intelligence is the most direct and present source of personal data; yet we often overlook it. The thoughts we think and the emotions we feel are second-order interpretations of body sensations. In other words, body intelligence is the original information. The mind can get lost in worries and regrets or stray into memories and plans. The heart can be distracted by hopes or fears or distorted with longing or loss. But the signals we receive from our bodies are always happening now. When we directly access body intelligence, nothing is lost in translation.

Often our mind chatter is so loud that listening to body intelligence is like straining to hear a whisper in a room where someone is screaming. There are many ways that we can increase sensitivity to our body's signals. Body scanning meditation is one way to practice this. In some Vipassana meditation traditions, practitioners are guided to pay attention to specific parts or areas of the body and asked to notice what is there.

Another way we can connect with body wisdom is through applied kinesiology. Using these techniques, we ask ourselves specific questions and learn to interpret the answers that we receive through real-time physical feedback. Creator of the reintegration system Nebo Lukovich describes two simple methods for conducting manual muscle testing on a yes-no question.

Option 1: Create a loop between your thumb and index finger on each hand as if you were making the sign language sign for "okay." Intertwine these two loops, as if they were links in a chain. Try to maintain the integrity of the loop of your non-dominant hand, while trying to break that same loop with your dominant hand. Meanwhile, keep your question in mind. If you are able to maintain the "okay" sign made by your non-dominant hand, then the answer to your question is "yes." If the loop of your non-dominant hand is broken, then the answer is "no."

Option 2: Create a loop between your thumb and index finger on your non-dominant hand, making an "okay" sign. Use the index finger of your dominant hand to test the strength of the loop. Put the index finger of the dominant hand into the "okay" sign made by your non-dominant hand and try to break it, while keeping your question in mind. If you are able to maintain the "okay" sign made by your non-dominant hand, then the answer to your question is "yes." If the loop of your non-dominant hand is broken, then the answer is "no."

Regularly engaging in this kind of body awareness practice can expand your capacity to receive the messages that your body is always sending you. There is a lot of deconditioning required here because we have largely been taught to ignore our body signals, to put "mind over matter" and push through the pain. Eventually, as you become more skilled, the messages will start to register in your awareness, even when you are not specifically focused on them.

Purpose practices for cultivating Responsiveness

Improvisational theater

We cultivate Responsiveness when we hold space for nonjudgmental, nonlinear exploration. If you have taken part in a brainstorming session, you know the main rule in the idea generation stage is that anything and everything is welcome. Absolutely everything. There are no bad ideas because it is a judgement-free zone. Suspending judgement makes it safe for people to freely express whatever comes. It helps us relax around performance anxiety and productivity pressure. We encourage inspiration by removing blocks to its expression.

One way to enter judgement-free exploration is by playing with improvisational theater. Many of us probably think of improv comedy when we hear the word improvisation. We don't need to be aspiring comedians to benefit from doing improv exercises though. At its core, improvisation is about building capacity for spontaneity. We are encouraged to move, or speak, or sound out whatever occurs to us in the moment without thinking. This raw, unedited expression can spark hilarity, but it is not pre-scripted or designed to be funny.

Theater actor, director, and teacher Jesai Jayhmes describes an exercise that he frequently uses as a warmup: "The group stands together in a circle. Each person identifies what feelings are alive in them and then with a spontaneous sound and movement gives expression to that 'state' of their being. The rest of the group repeats the movement, or sound, or feeling as precisely as possible. This continues around the circle until everyone has non-verbally checked in and had their expression played back."

He explains the benefits of this practice. "Improvisation encourages our responsiveness by requiring us to leap into the action without premeditation in front of others. We learn from our parents and school to limit our physical and vocal expressiveness to what is deemed appropriate. By the time we are adults, many have lost the natural ability to express freely through the body feelings such as joy, sadness, and anger. These exercises encourage the spontaneous expression of the body, mind, and emotions."

Improvisational theater is the practice of dropping our usual appropriateness or approval filters and expressing whatever comes. It connects us with our authentic truth and encourages us to share it out loud with little or no consideration for the outcome.

Drawing meditation

If participating in an improvisational theater group is not practical for you, you can find other ways to enter a judgement-free space on your own. Mandala drawing is one way to do this. This is a solo creative meditation that I have done on a regular basis over the past five years. You can practice it on your own, nearly anywhere, with nothing more than a notebook and a pen.

The mandala meditation is a simple practice.

- Start by drawing a straight line or curved line or shape that is oriented to a point near the middle of the page.

It can be anything! A teardrop. A triangle. A diamond. A wave. A dot.

- Rotate the paper and repeat the same mark at regular intervals until you complete a full circle and return to the point where you started.
- Then start again by making another line or shape that is connected to the first one.
- Again, repeatedly make this mark while rotating the page in a circle, until you return to the starting point. You can continue this process for a set amount of time or simply keep going until you feel that you are done.

This mandala meditation practice focuses on the process of drawing, not the outcome. There are three attitudes that define this practice. First, you draw the mandala step-by-step without any grand plan or design in mind. Second, you accept and integrate everything that happens, knowing that there are no mistakes. Finally, when you finish, you view and appreciate the unique beauty of the design you have created without judging it as good or bad.

With group improvisation, we confront fears of external judgement. Though sometimes our toughest critics are on the inside. The mandala meditation helps us get friendly with our inner judges' bench, so that when those voices come through, they shake us a little more gently.

Non-linear movement

The conditioning that constricts Creative Flow can also be broken down on a body-cellular level. In everyday life, most of our physical movement is directed and directional. We move because we are going somewhere or doing something. We have an intention for our movement. With this, we establish a loop of linear thinking and directional movement, which reinforce each other. If we want to interrupt that loop, we need to create intentional confusion by engaging our bodies in random unplanned motion; movement that is for no reason at all.

Non-linear yoga is a practice that supports this. Postural yoga, or asana-based yoga, is about putting our bodies into specific postures, which have a "correct" alignment. We put a foot here and a hand there and we twist our body to conform to a prescribed shape. There is a right way and a wrong way to do it. The teacher's role in postural yoga is to instruct and correct us. They may even come to us and use their hands to adjust us. With non-linear yoga, there is no right way or wrong way. The teacher's role in non-linear yoga is merely to provide guidance or offer suggestions for ways we can move our bodies. With non-linear yoga, students are ultimately led by their own impulses and intuition on how and what to move.

We can pull a similar thread from the growing global movement of ecstatic dance. The core principles for this community-based movement practice are: (1) Move however you wish. (2) No talking on the dance floor. (3) No drugs and alcohol. (4) No photo or video capture. (5) Respect yourself and one another. These guidelines are designed to make the ecstatic dance space a safe place for people to listen inward and explore themselves through movement. It is about moving our bodies with a focus on internal exploration rather than external appreciation.

Non-linear movement supports Responsiveness because it emphasizes the liberation of expression over conforming to a standard of excellence. It allows us to explore freedom of movement without judgement, which gives us the space to truly respond instead of merely react. It short-circuits the programming that dictates there is a right way and a wrong way, so we can embrace whatever emerges as being *our* way.

Purpose practices for cultivating Receptivity

Fill your heart with gratitude

One of the most simple and effective practices for accessing abundance is gratitude. Gratitude practice is a cornerstone of most life-coaching toolkits. The thing is, having a gratitude practice does not mean robotically writing down three things that you are thankful for in your journal every day. It might include that, but if you stop there, you are missing out on the full potential of this practice. Gratitude is most powerful when it touches our hearts.

We take a lot of things for granted. Our systems are wired to be more sensitive to loss than to gain, which is why there's truth to the adage, "You don't know what you've got until it's gone." One thing that can help us connect to gratitude is to imagine ourselves being *without* something that we already have. This could be anything: our comfortable home, our supportive partner, our language skills, or our stamina to hike long distances. Imagining what life would be like without these blessings can evoke a newfound appreciation for what is already here.

That said, genuine gratitude goes beyond making lists of what we are grateful for and doing imagination gymnastics. Practicing gratitude ultimately means practicing noticing. It is about slowing down enough to appreciate the gifts we receive every day — the little things that often pass us by. It is delighting in the smell of your lover's hair. It is savoring the first sip of your morning coffee. It is smiling at the joyful old woman who serves you *pad thai*. By noticing these little things, we broaden our awareness of the ways in which we are always supported.

Celebrate resourcefulness

Another way to experience gratitude is by celebrating resourcefulness. When we have limited material resources, we tend to get clever about doing more with what we have. We can make the money that we have *stretch*. We get what we need by thinking outside of the box.

We honor resourcefulness by seeing and celebrating the various ways we resource ourselves. Maybe there is an instance where we asked someone to help us out. We can recognize how that request required humility or courage, and pat ourselves on the back for showing up for it. Maybe there is a broken piece of furniture that we took care to repair instead of sending it to a landfill. We can applaud ourselves for making the effort. Maybe there was a discarded item of clothing, an empty container, or a toy that our kids have outgrown, and we managed to find a new use for the old thing. We can cheer ourselves on for our inventiveness.

We typically see resourcefulness as the kind of cleverness that comes from constraint. We diminish the power of resourcefulness by viewing it as a stroke of insight that only occurs to us when we are backed into a corner and have no other way out. The unfortunate thing about this view is that it presupposes a state of lack. We unconsciously perpetuate scarcity thinking when we treat our inventiveness as being a side effect of something that is missing. What we want to do instead is to celebrate resourcefulness as gratitude in practice.

Lynne Twist writes about the benefits of this perspective shift in *The Soul of Money*: "When we let go of trying to get more of what we don't really need, we free up an enormous amount of energy that has been tied up in the chase. We can refocus and reallocate that energy and attention towards appreciating what we already have, what's already there, and making a difference with that. Not just noticing it, but making a difference with what we already have. When you make a difference with what you have, it expands."

When we are resourceful, we appreciate and lovingly use the resources that we have. From an abundance point of view, resourcefulness is an expression of *resourced fullness*.

Nourish economic ecosystems

During the industrial revolution, millions moved to urban centers for education or employment, leaving behind their families and communities of origin. We sacrificed the social net of village life in exchange for the economic opportunities of city life. Fast forward a few hundred years. We see technology advancing, commerce going global, and cities getting bigger and denser. Now the feeling of disconnection is pervasive. We are a society of separate, independent individuals, competing against strangers who feel far removed from us in the public sphere.

The next step forward may seem like a step backward. It is recovering and reclaiming a sense of interdependence. We want to feel part of the global tapestry of humanity; we want to plug into the current of the human web. Social media is the addictive sugar-high substitution for the deeper, more nourishing connection that we crave. What many of us are really starving for is connection in a real-life community of exchange.

In Chinese culture, the community of exchange is characterized by *guanxi*. Simply translated, the term guanxi means relationship. But there is a texture to guanxi networks that is richer than mere relationship — it is a sense of relatedness marked by mutual respect, trust, commitment, and reciprocity. In a guanxi culture, familial norms of interactions extend beyond the immediate biological family. In Western culture, we typically judge the conflating of personal and business relationships as nepotism. That distortion is possible of course. However, business professor Peter Verhezen points out that it only turns into nepotism if the achievement of a result by leveraging a relationship becomes more important than the relationship itself.

The frequency of abundance is transmitted when we feel wholly supported. We access this feeling of universal support when we take part in communities of exchange. It helps to be living among people we know and feel known by; working with people we care about and feel cared for by. Abundance Flow is facilitated by a sense of connection to the family of humanity while we are giving and being given to, receiving and being received. Money is part of this, but it is only a part. The key here is that economic exchange is primarily oriented around community, and only secondarily around commerce. In other words, the personal connection between giver and receiver is what matters the most, not the amount of the financial transaction.

In the new paradigm, we want to foster "double positive" exchanges — multi-dimensional deals that create value in every act of exchange. In a conventional commercial exchange where we use money to purchase goods or services, the focus is not on creating value; it is on *extracting* value. If the price is set higher, the seller wins. If the price is set lower, the buyer wins. This sets up an adversarial dynamic between the two parties. It often ends with one person feeling like they got the better deal, and the other feeling taken advantage of.

In "double positive" exchanges, we exchange much more than just money. We generate value in the form of love, respect, appreciation, goodwill, esteem, reputation, testimonials, referrals, introductions, access to social networks, and so on. In these exchanges, both parties emerge feeling like they got the best deal. One person's sense of abundance does not have to diminish another's. The value that is created in this kind of exchange is more than the sum of its parts and it is unquantifiable. An overflowing sense of gratitude and generosity is available to all when we recognize that we are members of the same team, contributing to the same mission. We can give generously what feels easy to give without calculating, accounting, or withholding. We can gratefully receive everything we need and more.

With regenerative purpose, economic exchange is about building and enlivening, rather than buying and extracting. It puts community first, commerce second.

Acknowledgements

The rivers don't drink their own water. Trees don't eat
their own fruits. The Sun does not shine for itself. And
flowers do not spread their fragrance for themselves.
Living for others is a rule of nature.
— **Pope Francis**

We often say, "It takes a village." Yes, it's true. To realize big dreams, it requires the energy, the love, the power, the wisdom, the courage, the commitment, the conviction, and the resources of many people. At the same time, the process of creation *makes a village* too. That is what we have here.

By joining hearts and hands, we have assembled a virtual village. At the time of publication, nearly 300 people had come together around this book baby. I conclude my writing journey by returning to the beginning. Looking back on all the twists and turns in this adventure, I feel incredibly supported. And I am deeply touched to see so many hearts and so many hands, now connected in purpose.

The new paradigm of purpose embraces the truth of our *inter*dependence. It recognizes how we all suffer together or heal together, sink together or rise together.

Beyond supporting the life cycle of this book as a particular purpose form, what we are putting our collective energy behind is a movement. This movement is reshaping the way we think about our place in the world, and the way we engage in our work.

Thank you for tying a small boat of yours to mine. I am honored to be connected and creating with you as we rise together.

Collaborators

These collaborators are individuals who have invested their time, skills, and talents to the conception, creation, production, publication, and promotion of this book in a hands-on way. Without their heart work, this book simply would not exist in its current form.

- Ada H. Ko, cover design consultant - Instagram @tiffinstudio
- Alina Gutierrez, graphic artist and illustrator - visualversa.com
- Brian Gruber, writing coach and self-publishing mentor - grubermedia.com
- Gary Roberts, videographer for crowdfunding campaign - garyrobertsvideo.com
- Katie Brockhurst, social media coach - socialmediaforanewage.com
- Katie Mae Scripps, content and copy editor - Instagram @katiemaezing
- Kim Lijffijt, content and copy editor - Instagram @kimeisje
- Kirilly Sunshine, astrologer - kirilly.space
- Mia Renwall, vocal coach for audiobook - soundcloud.com/mia-renwall

- Miriam Ropschitz, editor and proofreader - miriamropschitz.com
- Sandeep Likhar, digital and print layout - likharpublishing.com
- Shivan Bruce Skipper, photographer and design consultant - radical-clarity.com
- Zlatina Zareva, graphic designer - zeedidsee.com

Contributors

These contributors have freely and generously shared their ideas, insights, and words of wisdom with me during the writing process. They are people whom I have personally interviewed on the themes in the book. Their personal narratives and perspectives have been important in shaping the content and context shared within these pages.

- Amanda Johnson, author mentor and authentic writing guide - amandajohnson.tv
- Anais Bock, originator of the four-part purpose Venn diagram - letsworkmagic.com
- Ann Liu, painter, intimacy blogger and community builder - anahata.studio
- Brandon Peele, purpose guide, author, and speaker - brandonpeele.com
- Daan Gorter, social entrepreneurship mastermind creator - tribepreneurs.com
- David Atherton, Japanese scholar and Harvard professor of East Asian studies
- Ezra S. Bell, web developer and business strategist, Appointlet

- Francesco W. Marcuccio, conscious-business coach - francescomarcuccio.com
- Irena Ateljevic, founder of Sibenik Hub for Ecology - shebenik.com
- James Hady, somatic trauma therapist and shadow integration guide
- James P. Sloan, head of platform product, LiveRamp
- Jesai Jayhmes Burnett, actor, director and theater teacher - jeffburnettonbroadway.com
- Jessica Montalvo, physician and functional medicine expert - mindwisehealthcare.com
- Katie Mae Scripps, sacred sexuality educator and social change performance artist
- Kim Lijffijt, education specialist, conscious relating enthusiast, and evolutionary life guide
- Matteo Ottaviani, climate research scientist, Terra Research Inc.
- Martha Tara Lee, clinical sexologist and relationship counselor - eroscoaching.com
- Michael Duff, chief information security officer, Stanford University
- Nehal Vadhan, research and clinical psychologist in addictions - bit.ly/nehal-vadhan
- Nick Williams, inspired leadership guide and author - iamnickwilliams.com

Supporters

In April 2019, my friends, friends of friends, family members, former classmates, former colleagues, and a few anonymous strangers, donated a total of $11,121 to a crowdfunding campaign to support the creation of this book. Many gave generously, not only money, but also heartfelt words of encouragement along the way. In one month, we raised enough money to cover most of the expenses associated with publishing and launching the first edition. The entire sum of funds raised was passed through to pay for the professional services of those named in the collaborators group above. As a self-published and self-funded author, this financial and emotional support was critical for getting this book from concept into physical form.

Jessica Montalvo, Michael Duff, James Sloan, Lucy Caldwell, Martin Burns, Whit Collier, Mimi Ben Otman, Phyllis Tam, Rob McKerlie, Jo Jo Walsh, Linda Walter, Alexis Tapia, Warren Shu, Lindsey Coleman, Magdalena Romo, Veronica Aguirre, John Pihlblad, Katie T. Larson, Gavin Clayworth, Miriam Ropschitz, Lindsay Adams, Orly Faya Snir, Alison Downey, Edna Bian, Joe Allen, Julie Moksim, Mike Sowden, Marie Poland, Patricia Ruzicka, Stacey Griner, Melissa Rutz, Julia Schreck, Satyama Lasby, Lena Wegener, Sophie Sabrina Sharp, Parinaz Kermani, Kaichun Lu, Franklin Lu, Wendy Lin, Summer Estes, Elissa Windisch, Stu Shapley, Russ Hudson, Kelly Turgeon, Stephen Ueng, Michael Franklin, Erin Eriksson, Valeska Maria Fischer, Henna Minhas Garg, Leonard Lee, Peter Schreck, Hung-Yuan Lin, Brian Gruber, Hilary Kimball, Michael Ueng, Ardeshir Mehran, Eileen O'Connor, Mallory Elliott, Leah Johnson, David Barnosky, Tushar Tanna, Damon Magnuski, Sarvaan Ziva, Ada Ko, Katie Mae Scripps, Nick Fowler, Angela Roster, Jennifer Wagner, Kitty Willis, Rita Ho-Bezzola, Mai Hope Le, Catriona Jessamy, Kristin Karu, Tanja Wessels, Susan Lucci, David Atherton, Nicole Mason, Jill

Davis, Marian Kleine, Tracy McNeil, Matthew Henkler, Sylwia Dzuman, Kim Lijffijt, Liz Dowling, Amanda Johnson, Tisha Gomes, Evan Brandon, David Major, Brandon Peele, Caroline Kim, Caroline Kaufmann, Daniel Stec, Shana Pallotta, Aleta Spitaleri, Kelsey Lotus Wong, Missy Kroninger, Zee Johnson, Lauren Anshutz, Rick Albrink, Ella Daniela, Tien Luong, Shannon Tracey, Allison Marshall, Plia Pesya, Deborah Jane, Pete Jensen, Clemens-Michael Kluge, Sally Ann Jones, Jamilah Preenun Nana, Sara Mahdavi, Stacey Stieglitz, David Konis, Gosia Anna Sereda, Nathalie Joel-Smith, Mary Elizabeth Murphy, Darren Smith, Matteo Morozzo, Anh Nguyen, Miranda Malloy, Amra Kolenovic, Abraham Drucker, Ivan Kepecs, Andrew Marshall, Martha Tara Lee, Samantha Skye, Rose Evans Walker, Sunny Ju, Valerie Tih, Ken Cutts, Cathy Baird, Natasha Fong, Kobi Ben Zaken, Jay Su, Ronald Leung, Athena Pallis, Alina Gutierrez, Anne McFadden, Anouk Hornman, Gabriela Moriarty, Lisbeth Jorgensen, Ananda Lowrey, Jason Burak, Jan Nicholas, Pauline Cheung, Nynke Marije Feenstra, Elli Zissi Iconomou, Kim Dubois, Amanda Garvin, Faith Hill, Yvonne Yam, Jessica Huntington, Dave E. Lee, Arjun Chahal, Virginie Patard, Julien Hawthorne, Annu Kristipati, Patrick Shannon, Nathalie Assarf, Therese Helland, Karin Rodenbach, Leslie Mallman, Brandy Haiman, Tracy Fong, Winnie Li, Phyllis Rawley, Jonian Grazhdani, Laura Vroom, Rob Weber, Alisa Blundon, Justin Lee, Martina Etemadieh, Kerah Cottrell, Mark Wasiljew, Peter Schmidt, Yulia Kurlyaninova, Jessica McCarthy, Anne Kurth, Gloria Tam, Tania Sahai, Svetlana Kim, Sonia Dominguez, Joshua Fields, Max Shkud, Alona Movenko, Andrea Dennis, Marie Hentschel, Raymond Codina, Ali Binazir, Veronica Radin, Rosa

C. Leal, Ipek Serifsoy, Kirilly Sunshine, Triz Green, David Llorca, Andra Saimre, Emily Moyer, Angie K. Millgate, Ann Liu, Christine Southworth, Vanessa Deering, Hilary Zalon, Nimisha Gandhi, Anny Lee, Todd Brown, Irina Busurina, Beverley Leemann, Katie Brockhurst, Kim Lasinger, Jennifer Li, Alexandra Abdel-Malek, Anna Sainclivier, Prem Rasa, Raquel Figueiroa, Mirjam Irene, Mel Lowe, Michelle Unique, Grace Farrelly, Danielle Frankel, Stefan Schaubitzer, Shay Barbalat, Christabelle Moonshine, Matteo Ottaviani, Kim Mitchell Stokes, Sarra Hedden, Paal Christian Buntz, Elodie Labonne, Pascal Van der Elst, Anne Johnson, Jonathon David Dickson Fisher, James Marriott, Hubert Huot

Invitation to support this work

If you want to express gratitude for *Regenerative Purpose* and its impact on your life by giving a donation, you can do that here: paypal.me/heywendymay

Monetary gifts of any amount are welcome. Personal notes about how this book has touched you are also much appreciated. Your financial and emotional support provide energy for me to regenerate as I keep going on my purpose path.

About the Author

Wendy May is a Regenerative Purpose path-light and purpose activist. A Harvard alumna with a graduate business degree from UCLA, Wendy started on her own purpose path after leaving a 15-year corporate career in leadership development and organizational consulting. Through her writing, speaking, coaching and programs, Wendy facilitates deep purpose alignment processes to help create a world of work that works for everyone.

Connect with Wendy May at heywendymay.com or follow her on social media @heywendymay on Facebook, Instagram, LinkedIn and Medium.